To Chum—
Take care!
Anne Jackson

D0381988

PRAISE FOR MAD CHURCH DISEASE

Anne Jackson has taken the problem by the jugular and brings remedy. Infused with a lively and informative style, *Mad Church Disease* is a life-saving resource for anyone in ministry—vocational or volunteer—who would like to understand, prevent, or treat the epidemic of burnout in church culture.

> —Dr. Wayne Cordeiro, senior pastor, New Hope Christian Fellowship, Honolulu, Hawaii, and author of *The Divine Mentor*

Anne Jackson is the real deal. And I appreciate her honest approach to a touchy topic. *Mad Church Disease* is a must-read for anyone who has gotten burned or burned-out by the church.

> —Mark Batterson, lead pastor, National Community Church, Washington, D.C., and author of *Wild Goose Chase*

This oft-ignored disease of the church is compromising the overall health of the American church. We've all had a touch of it—some have succumbed to it. This book hits the nail on the head clearly and does so with hope. Every minister should read *Mad Church Disease*—not just once, but from time to time.

> —Bob Roberts Jr., senior pastor, NorthWood Church, Keller, Texas, and author of *The Multiplying Church*

Every Christian leader intends to "finish our race well." Yet far too many of us end up escaping into sin or becoming numb, embittered, and angry. *Mad Church Disease* offers all of us the hope that we can actually make it to the end of the race, loving God and others with greater passion and being filled with audacious joy. Anne Jackson writes with raw honesty and hard-earned wisdom from her own story of burnout.

> —Nancy Beach, teaching pastor, Willow Creek Community Church, South Barrington, Illinois, and author of *Gifted to Lead*

My first thought: "What does a twenty-eight-year-old know about burnout?" Then I read this story about a girl named Anne, who grew up in a pastor's home and has lived through enough experiences to know what she's talking about. Anne Jackson not only tells her own story, but she gracefully integrates principles that have me at times saying, "That's right!" and at other times admitting, "That's me." As soon as I can, I'll be ordering enough copies for our entire staff.

> —Tim Stevens, executive pastor, Granger Community Church, Granger, Indiana, and author of *Pop Goes the Church*

From the perspective of her own devastating personal experience, as well as by means of strongly researched facts, Anne Jackson opens our eyes to the crisis of ministry burnout. This paralyzing and contagious condition has wounded so many in church leadership. *Mad Church Disease* is a light on the path to healing and health.

— Nancy Ortberg, author of *Unleashing the Power of Rubber Bands*

I cannot say enough about how important the ideas put forth in *Mad Church Disease* are. With refreshing humility, grace, and transparency, Anne Jackson reveals the realities of burnout and how we can avoid being infected by this vicious disease. If you truly want to thrive and survive in ministry, this book is a must-read.

— Mike Foster, president of Ethur and author of *Deadly Viper Character Assassins*

Burned-out leaders are heading up the mass exodus out of the inherited church. Anne Jackson's book *Mad Church Disease* brings much-needed attention to the dark compulsions of celebrity-driven churches that abuse and spew out our best people. But it does more than that. It also offers hope through stories of survival, pertinent scriptural teaching, and the prescription of a balanced, healthy, holistic lifestyle that will ensure longevity and the kind of joyful service that leaves no casualties. I wish I had read this book ten years ago. My family wishes I had read it twenty years ago!

— Andrew Jones, blogger at Tall Skinny Kiwi, tallskinnykiwi.typepad.com

The issues that Anne Jackson explores in *Mad Church Disease* are central to every church staff and every pastor's family. Having been both a church staff member and a pastor's kid, I'm thankful for her honesty and courage. Well done!

— Shauna Niequist, author of *Cold Tangerines*

If you're in ministry or thinking about going into ministry, *Mad Church Disease* is required reading. With grace and hope, Anne Jackson sheds some much-needed light on the dirty politics, emotional abuse, and physical burnout that are plaguing leadership in today's churches. Thankfully, Jackson's "disease" isn't terminal. Her book will help ministers of all shapes and sizes pursue God's work in a healthy, passionate, and creative environment.

— Matthew Paul Turner, author of *Churched: One Kid's Journey Toward God Despite a Holy Mess*

MAD CHURCH DISEASE

OVERCOMING THE BURNOUT EPIDEMIC

ANNE JACKSON

ZONDERVAN®

ZONDERVAN.com/
AUTHORTRACKER
follow your favorite authors

ZONDERVAN®

Mad Church Disease
Copyright © 2009 by Anne Jackson

Requests for information should be addressed to:

Zondervan, *Grand Rapids, Michigan* 49530

Library of Congress Cataloging-in-Publication Data
    Jackson, Anne, 1980 –
        Mad church disease : overcoming the burnout epidemic / Anne Jackson.
           p. cm.
        Includes bibliographical references.
        ISBN 978-0-310-28755-1 (hardcover)
        1. Burn out (Psychology) – Religious aspects – Christianity. I. Title.
    BV4509.5.J325 2009
    253 – dc22   2008027412

All Scripture quotations, unless otherwise indicated, are taken from the *Holy Bible, New International Version*®. NIV®. Copyright © 1973, 1978, 1984 by International Bible Society. Used by permission of Zondervan. All rights reserved.

Internet addresses (websites, blogs, etc.) and telephone numbers printed in this book are offered as a resource to you. These are not intended in any way to be or imply an endorsement on the part of Zondervan, nor do we vouch for the content of these sites and numbers for the life of this book.

All rights reserved. No part of this publication may be reproduced, stored in a retrieval system, or transmitted in any form or by any means — electronic, mechanical, photocopy, recording, or any other — except for brief quotations in printed reviews, without the prior permission of the publisher.

Published in association with the literary agency of Alive Communications, Inc., 7680 Goddard Street, Suite 200, Colorado Springs, CO 80920. www.alivecommunications.com

Interior design by Ben Fetterley

Printed in the United States of America

09 10 11 12 13 14 • 22 21 20 19 18 17 16 15 14 13 12 11 10 9 8 7 6 5 4 3

"Never give up on church."
I leaned in close to his face as my grandfather whispered those words
hours before he passed away.
Those were the last five words he spoke to me.
At the time, I had no idea the weight those words would someday carry.

This book is dedicated to you, Grandpa Emmett.

And I promise I won't.

THE FINE PRINT

The stories in this book are all true. When needed, those named or those who are able to represent them have given me permission to use their stories. For those who were unavailable to contact, irrelevant details of the anecdotes and names have been changed to protect their identity.

I am not a doctor of any specialty, and the content in this book does not constitute medical or psychological advice. Where necessary, please use your best judgment and consult medical professionals when embarking on your journey to health.

Thank you.

CONTENTS

FOREWORD

Years ago, during a particularly low time in my life and ministry, I sat in a leadership conference hoping for something — anything — that would relieve the pain I felt so deeply.

I loved Jesus, but his church was wearing me out.

One of my ministry heroes, Bill Hybels, took the stage. As usual, I was mesmerized by his wisdom, passion, and authenticity. Without my ever seeing it coming, God blindsided me with some of Bill's words. I'll never forget the chills that shot down my spine the moment Bill explained his dilemma. Through sincere pain and an obvious desire to change, Bill openly confessed that "the way I was doing the work of God was destroying the work of God in my life."

That was it. Someone had finally put words to what I felt so deeply. The *way* I was doing the work of God was destroying the work of God in me. Something had to change.

Why is it that the ones who are called to minister to others are often so dysfunctional? Why is it that those who help others heal are often so sick? Why is Jesus so loving and his church so difficult?

This week I had a conversation with a close pastor-friend. He confided in me the story that I've heard from ministers way too many times. He is miserable, hurting, exhausted, depleted — and flirting with spiritual burnout.

I've been praying for him for a long time. I am asking God that he keep my gifted friend from becoming another statistic — another broken pastor who crawls away from the church and his "calling," simply trying to survive and rebuild his life.

Something is wrong with the way many ministers minister.

Thankfully, in *Mad Church Disease*, Anne has courageously exposed her story, hurts, fears, and disappointments. This candid, humorous book will have you laughing, crying, groaning — and ultimately healing.

I am genuinely excited that you are reading this book. Or more accurately, that this book might be reading you. If you are a wounded spiritual warrior, I believe that God will use Anne's story and wisdom to initiate healing in your life. If you are a young and hungry minister, it will empower you to avoid many of ministry's dangerous land mines.

No matter what your context, your time in the exam room is approaching. God might diagnose you with a common ministry illness called "mad church disease." The great news is that he will bring healing through the book you hold in your hands.

— Craig Groeschel, founding and senior pastor, LifeChurch.tv

HOW TO USE THIS BOOK

Toward the end of selected chapters, you'll find something called "Exam Room." This feature contains questions designed for you to do what you would do in any doctor's exam room — strip down and get naked about what's making you sick.

WRITE DOWN YOUR ANSWERS.

And discuss.

Also, as anyone will tell you, always ask for a second opinion. I've made that part easy by including interviews I've done with leaders whom I deeply respect. You'll gain wisdom from their thoughts about and experiences of burnout.

PROLOGUE: NO PITY PARTIES HERE

Growing up, pity parties were my specialty. If my younger brother got a bigger present than I got at Christmas or if I didn't get cast as the lead in my school play, I would get really down on myself. I'd lock myself in my bedroom and cry and cry and cry.

"Why me?"

When we run into obstacles we don't expect in life, it's easy to end up in that "Why me?" state of mind. It's extremely tempting to focus on the negative. After all, it isn't fair. It isn't what we had planned, and it screws everything up.

I've heard thousands of stories from people who have been hurt by the church. People who have given so much and asked for so little in return. They run and run and run until they collapse. Staff members, families, and volunteers. Men, women, and even children. The pain doesn't discriminate with regard to position, gender, or age.

And it's not fair.

> And it does hurt.

There's a painful side to burnout we're not going to ignore.

However, locking ourselves in our bedrooms and focusing on all that's wrong in this world isn't going to do us — or the people who are entrusted to us — any good.

We've got to face the future

> with courage, hope, grace, and love —

> > regardless of our circumstances.

We have to heal.

We have to be healthy.

I hope that together we will be able to align health and responsibility in a way that will illuminate the power and glory of the One who created us.

INTRODUCTION

All of us are on a unique journey. No two stories are the same. Chances are, if you picked up this book, you and I share some common threads in our tapestries.

Burnout is a disease nobody talks about until it's too late. Statistics and stories prove that the health of those serving in ministry is declining — spiritually, physically, emotionally, and relationally.

At some point along the road, your heart, your mind, your spirit — maybe even your body — have been damaged while fighting the battles of good and evil.

Mine too.

When we should have been fighting with our fellow believers back-to-back, we find ourselves bandaging our wounds from friendly fire.

When we should be breathing life into a comatose world, we find ourselves gasping for air, just trying to survive.

When we should be celebrating the gift of our friends and families, we find our hearts breaking for the way they are mistreated.

A very real pain comes out of a very real battle each of us is called to fight. To some of us, this is a relatively new and shocking pain. To others, we've grown numb because we've learned to expect the worse.

You may be taking your first steps into serving. Or maybe like me, you've been exposed to both the beautiful and terrible faces of the church for your entire life.

Although our stories may be different, we are unified in at least one very clear and very special way.

It is obvious that God has placed a burden on your heart to see the church, and the world, healed and restored.

Me too.

So I wanted to share a little bit of my own background, with the intent that you'll not only get to know the woman behind the words but also relate to some part of my life — whether my childhood, my time away from the church, my own "crash and burn," or even that exciting feeling of the Spirit stirring in your heart.

HI. I'M ANNE, AND I WAS BORN IN A CHURCH

Even before my dad was a pastor, we pretty much spent every waking moment at church. My mom was in the choir, my dad taught various classes, and I hung out in the nursery with the other sippy cup-toting toddlers.

When I was five, my father took a pastoral position at a small church in Circle Back, Texas. It was his first full-time position out of seminary, and he got paid a stately $200 per week. My mother stayed at home and took care of my baby brother. On weekends, my dad and I would go fishing or rock hunting.

Everything seemed normal. We were a happy pastor's family.

At least for a little while.

A few years later, we moved to a farming community in west Texas. Although my father's paycheck was only slightly more, his time away from our family had exponentially increased. He'd come home later and later at night. He was tired. Although we'd still go fishing, our plans seemed to be interrupted more often than not.

Once a month, he'd have a deacons meeting. I began noticing that when he came home from these particular meetings, he'd be upset. He'd make sure my brother and I were in bed before he and my mom would have closed-door discussions.

Some might call it being nosy, but I like to call it "being curious." Even after using the "glass to the wall" trick I had seen on television, I could never make out specific words of my parents' conversations. But the tone was unmistakable.

Something was terribly wrong, and I needed to know what it was.

With my mom having begun to teach to supplement our income and my dad always being gone, I was responsible for taking care of my younger brother. I'd give him some Ninja Turtles to keep him occupied, and I'd begin to pore over my Nancy Drew books.

Why?

I had a mystery to solve. And I needed to learn how to spy.

I began setting up an infallible plan to listen in on the next deacons meeting.

DEACONS MEETING ESPIONAGE

The meetings always took place in the fellowship hall, and much to my benefit, there was a janitor's closet adjacent to the room. I had another thing working for me. There was an exterior door that opened into the janitor's closet.

Over the next week, I snuck into the church and began building a small fort of tables in the corner of the janitor's closet. I angled the tables so that when I entered the closet through the exterior door, I'd be completely hidden.

The Sunday of the deacons meeting approached. During the morning service, I left the auditorium to use the bathroom, making another stop along the way. I put my spy kit — a Trapper Keeper folder with a photo of two kittens on it, my favorite four-colored pen, and a small tape recorder — underneath the tables. I also unlocked the exterior door, ensuring I'd be able to easily enter the room later that evening.

I could barely contain my excitement that day, anticipating my mission that night. I went home after the services and told my mom I was going to bed early. She eventually went outside to the utility room to do laundry.

That's when I made my escape.

I swiftly traveled from our parsonage to the church next door and quietly entered through the exterior door to the janitor's closet.

My plan was perfect.

The meeting had just started, and I could hear everyone's voice clearly. I pressed the *play+record* combination on the tape recorder, just to make sure I didn't miss anything.

One of the four deacons said an opening prayer. Another began the meeting by summarizing the previous month's attendance and finances and giving updates on hospitalized members who had been visited.

Boring ...

I began doodling on my paper until I heard my dad mention the word *vacation*.

"Well, the kids are heading back to school next month, and since my father's cancer is spreading, I thought I'd take my yearly vacation in a few weeks to have the family visit my parents in Fort Worth."

Sweet! I love staying with my grandparents! Please say yes, please say yes, please say yes.

The room was unexpectedly quiet. I heard a metal folding chair squeak, and a deacon, who was also the music director, said in an angry, thick Texas accent, "Brother Ron, now, you know you already took your vacation back in May when you went to Russia. You can't expect for us to be alright with you takin' another one."

My dad paused, then replied, "The trip to Russia? Brother Chuck, that was an association mission trip. You know that. My family didn't go."

Brother Chuck didn't seem too impressed. He growled, "Still sounds like a vacation to me!"

One thing I've always loved about my dad is the deliberately slow and patient tone with which he speaks. Even in the most ridiculous situations, he manages to keep an almost frighteningly calm demeanor.

"If you consider visiting a Communist nation and being followed by the KGB as you try to discreetly hand out Bibles a vacation, I suppose you're correct."

Oh. So that's where I get my spiritual gift of sarcasm.

I could hear the other deacons begin to grumble. The lead deacon who moderated the meeting interrupted the next livid remark Brother Chuck was beginning to make. "Chuck, you know very well it was a church-sponsored and approved mission trip. Brother Ron, I hope you and your family have a great time visiting your folks. Let's move on."

My fourth grade brain couldn't comprehend what had just happened. I knew adults disagreed, but this was our music leader. I had never heard him speak so angrily, and I didn't understand why only one of the deacons had defended my father. I thought these people were his friends!

I didn't have much time to dwell on these thoughts before Chuck started talking again. This time, however, his words came from left field.

"You know, Brother Ron. *You* are a liar."

EXCUSE ME? I almost flew out of the janitor's closet and punched Chuck in his face. My heart began pounding, and I desperately wanted to defend my dad.

I took a deep breath and managed to stay put. A good spy never lets emotions get in the way of the mission.

My dad, seemingly unfazed by this remark, asked what would lead Chuck to make such a terrible accusation.

Chuck replied, "I saw you park your cars on the church parking lot instead of on your driveway this weekend. You're trying to make it look like we've got more people here — and we can't have a liar for a pastor. So I'm going to ask you to resign at the next business meeting."

My dad reminded Chuck of the landscaping being done at the parsonage and that the cars had to be moved out of our driveway until it was taken care of. The church had approved the expense and the work a few months ago.

Chuck mumbled something about how he must have missed that meeting.

After dealing with a few other minor issues, the group began a time of prayer to close out the meeting. I closed up shop and left. Checking to make sure my mom was in my parents' bedroom as I predicted her to be, I came through the side door and managed to get into my bedroom undetected.

A few minutes later, my dad came home, exhausted. I heard him ask if we were in bed as he closed the door to their room. Through the walls I could hear my mom cry as Dad shared the meeting's "highlights."

I didn't sleep much that night. My heart was still racing, and my stomach felt a little sick from hearing people who were supposedly closest to my dad tear him apart and refuse to come to his defense. These were Christian men. I went to school with their children. We would eat at their homes, and they'd come over to ours.

A little bit of my world crashed in on me that night.

And I wish I would have known that this night was only the beginning.

A FIERY ESCAPING TO A FIRE ESCAPE

Needless to say, things only got worse at that church. My father eventually resigned and took another pastoring position in a town two hours away.

I was thirteen and had fallen back into the role of the good preacher's kid. The church seemed healthy, my dad was home more, and I assumed we'd be there for a very long time. I remember my dad saying he thought he could retire from this church.

Three years later, another hopeful circumstance turned ugly.

One night, my dad received a phone call from Stanley, one of his closest friends and mentors, who also happened to be a deacon. He told my father that an impromptu leaders meeting had been called earlier that day — and my dad had intentionally not been invited. Stanley had gone to the meeting because he knew that the man who organized it had a tendency to stir up trouble in the church, and he wanted to be there to bring some balance.

The issue was evangelism — kind of. My father is very passionate about evangelism and outreach to the community. He had planned several classes for members to learn why and how somebody shares Christ. Over three-quarters of the people in the town we were living in didn't go to church — so the stakes for life change were huge!

However, a younger group of leaders in the church believed that because my dad was being paid to do ministry, his attempts to get the entire church involved in outreach was only "slacking off." They made similar accusations toward our youth pastor.

My dad realized that his options were limited.

A few months later, at a regularly scheduled business meeting, my dad read a letter to the church announcing his "forced" resignation.

He said nobody was holding a gun to his head, but his love for unity was forcing him to step down. He told the members about the issues that, if not dealt with, would cause a split, and because he cared more for their health as a body, he was going to step away from this ministry.

A few members asked questions and told my father he didn't need to leave. Most of the church sat quietly, with deer-in-the-headlights looks on their faces. The core group of antagonists began to make absurd threats about what they'd do to my family if my dad didn't step down. A few stood up and defended his outreach plans.

It became a very messy meeting.

The feeling of frustration I had experienced several years prior had quickly returned, and it was now coupled with teenage angst and courage. Armed with years of Awana and Bible drills, I quickly flipped to Ephesians 4:3, stood up, interrupted what was going on, cleared my throat loudly, and read, *"Make every effort to keep the unity of the Spirit through the bond of peace."*

I continued in a shaky voice. "How can you even call yourselves Christians when all you do is fight? This is just ... *stupid!"*

I was met with a mixture of apathy and silence. I closed my Bible, picked up the notebook I always kept with me, and stormed out, slamming the large wooden door behind me. As quickly as I could, I ran over to our education building and climbed the fire escape. Under the glow and buzz of a nearby streetlight, I furiously wrote a letter to God in my journal with the small, golf scorecard pencil I had gotten out of the back of a pew.

I gave God a choice that night (sixteen-year-olds are so smart!). Either I was going to part ways with the church entirely, or he was going to give me a way to help bring unity to the church. I'll admit that it was a big prayer for a sixteen-year-old. And I'm not quite sure how I knew what it all meant. I just knew that my heart had been set on fire — and if God would let me, my sole purpose in life had just been defined.

So I waited.

SILENCE

I didn't receive an answer that night, or really anytime shortly thereafter, so I assumed God didn't care. After my father resigned, my family moved to Dallas so we could be closer to my aging grandparents and so my mom could take a teaching job.

Several months after moving, my dad still hadn't found employment. He would occasionally look for jobs, but because he was so burned-out from ministry, none of the ones he applied for were in a church. And I'm sure that many of you know that finding a job in the marketplace is nearly impossible after having difficulty defining your role in a church. He was clearly depressed. My dad spent most of his time in his bedroom. The spark in his eyes was gone.

Going to church was a very rare occurrence. The heaviness in our house was palpable.

How could the church do this? How could God let this happen?

Seeing the state of my family — both financially and emotionally — broke my heart even more. When I was seventeen, I decided to graduate from high school a year early and then moved out. I didn't want to be a burden financially. I turned down a few scholarships, decided not to go to college, and instead worked full-time managing a Christian bookstore.

But that was all a front. I was an empty shell, thinking my good-girl exterior would compensate for my dying heart. In the shadows of my life, I was medicating years of hurt by escaping. I slowly became addicted to pornography, which led to having inappropriate relationships, and I even began combining alcohol with prescription anxiety medicine — all to numb the pain I was feeling from my past experiences with church and other failed relationships.

After seeing even more brokenness in my job with the Christian bookstore, I decided I was through with anything "Jesus." I got a job working at a trendy Dallas dot-com. The new job only fueled my need and my ability to find resources for medicating my hurt. I couldn't bear the pain of my past — or the person I was allowing myself to become.

HINTS OF A SAVIOR

In the middle of this downward spiral, Julie, my best friend from high school, and I unexpectedly reconnected. Julie decided that she needed to take a break from college, and she moved into my Dallas condo.

The very first Sunday after she had moved in, she woke me up at the crack of dawn and asked me where I went to church.

I covered my head up with my duvet and told her to go to hell.

She decided to find a church on her own. By the time she came back, I was barely pulling myself out of bed.

"You're coming with me next week, OK?"

I repeated my earlier sentiment.

God definitely had Julie there for a reason. She slowly began to infuse our relationship with a Christlike love and grace. Although she let me know she couldn't stand to watch me do all the things I was doing, she was always there to make sure I was OK.

Through a mutual friend, we met a youth pastor who worked at a church a couple of hours away on the Texas/Oklahoma border. Even though it was a bit of a drive, Julie and I began attending his church every other Sunday. The youth pastor took a genuine interest in some of the issues I had been facing.

And can I be honest? He was single. And he was cute.

I felt I could trust him, so I opened up. He emailed me certain Scriptures he was praying for me, and I felt my heart beginning to soften. I quit drinking and stopped hanging out with some of the people who weren't the best influence in my life. I left my job at the dot-com and took a much more focused position at a design agency.

For the first time in a long time, I began giving in to the gentle songs God had begun to sing to my heart.

TOTO, WE'RE IN KANSAS

Julie and I continued attending the church in Oklahoma, and even though their charismatic methodology was much different from my traditional Baptist upbringing, God was clearly moving, and the small taste of what I experienced gave me the slightest bit of hope.

Five months after Julie moved to Dallas, I found out that my department at work was being downsized and my job was going to be eliminated within a few weeks.

I talked to Julie about the situation, and she suggested we move to Kansas for a fresh start.

The Midwest seemed safe and cheap enough. We had some friends in the Kansas City area. A week after my last day at the agency, we packed everything in a friend's van and my little sports car and headed up to the Sunflower State.

Since we were new, it was easy to blow off the church thing again. I had to find a job and become acquainted with the new city, right?

Several months after we had moved, some friends of ours who were in a band were playing at a church near our new apartment. We decided to go and hear them play.

The moment I stepped into the church, my heart started pounding and my stomach tightened up into an uncomfortable little ball. I couldn't breathe. I started to sweat.

Julie went up near the stage, but I stayed in the back of the auditorium. I sat hidden in a corner and tried to figure out what was happening. Was I sick? Was I having a panic attack? Maybe I had just had too much coffee.

IT'S NOT THE COFFEE

Remember the ultimatum I gave God on the fire escape?

Almost five years later, I got my answer.

I want you here. This is my church. This is my bride. Remember your father? Remember your pain? This is my church. This is my bride. I want you here. I will give you what you need. I will open up doors. And now is your time, if you'll let me. I want you here.

At the age of twenty-one, I was officially freaked out. And evidently, I was wearing my feelings on my sleeve.

A spunky redheaded girl around my age came up to me. She stuck out her hand. I shook it, still in shock from what I had just heard.

"Hi, I'm Kristi."

I think I told her my name.

"So can I pray with you?"

I stared up at her, dazed, and must have nodded my head yes.

She pulled me behind a partition and prayed for me. She prayed for a difficult situation I was having with my friends. She prayed for my relationship with Chris (my husband now — we had just started dating then).

And then she prayed for my involvement with the church.

What? My heart began pounding even harder. *Why would she say that?*

Kristi said amen and then asked the million-dollar question.

"So I work here at this church, and I really think you'd make a great table leader for our youth group. Interested?"

I politely declined.

Coming up with reasons to avoid church was completely second nature to me. I told her I hadn't been to church much in the last few years and was probably not the best example for students. I was really busy with my new job and would hate to overcommit.

She smiled, said she understood, and then asked if I'd mind having coffee with her sometime. We exchanged numbers, and within a few weeks we were hanging out pretty regularly.

After a little while, Kristi twisted my arm, and I agreed to help her out for one night at the church.

That one night turned into a year of volunteering.

And that year of volunteering turned into a full-time job offer in the student ministry where I had been serving.

Once again, I declined the offer. I was in the middle of planning my wedding, and I wanted to focus on my career and on my transition into being a new wife. My preference was to continue serving as a volunteer.

But I left out one very important reason.

I had promised myself that I would never, ever, EVER work in a church.

NEVER SAY NEVER

A couple of months after turning down the job, and just a month after getting married, I was hit with a virus that kept me in bed for almost two straight weeks. With nothing to do but lie flat on my back (we were too broke to have cable TV or Internet), I felt this unrelenting impression that I needed to call Chad, our student pastor, and talk to him about the job.

I picked up my phone, dialed, and hung up.

I just couldn't do it.

I was terrified to work at a church.

I could not take a chance and be hurt again. So deeply, deeply hurt.

As I reached to put my phone back on my night table, it rang.

It was Chad.

We talked about the position — about some of my reservations, but mostly about how, over the last two weeks, both of us were completely positive I was supposed to accept this role in ministry.

Even though I was so scared that I could have thrown up all over the place, I accepted the job.

I said yes.

I knew my life would never be the same.

PART I

HOW THE **BURNOUT EPIDEMIC** IS KILLING **THE GREATEST CALL**

CHAPTER 1

COMPARING MAD COW DISEASE TO MAD CHURCH DISEASE

In front of me sat a large pile of cattle carcasses, still smoldering from the fire that had essentially destroyed them. Occasionally, I'd hear a crackle or pop coming from the heap, but for the most part, the grassy English field was silent.

Thankfully, I was four thousand miles away, cozied up in my apartment and watching this on TV, far removed from the smells that would have been carried by the damp winds. I was tuned in to a BBC channel, viewing a documentary about bovine spongiform encephalopathy, an affliction better known as mad cow disease.

Now, mad cow disease is a pretty odd ailment that, for the most part, only infects cows. And, as I would learn in the documentary, it has four unique characteristics:

1. The disease lies dormant for a given amount of time, going unnoticed. It can be a period of months to a few years before the disease is found.

2. Mad cow disease is caused by a mutated protein that attaches itself to the cow's central nervous system, thus affecting the cow's brain and responses (hence the name). Essentially, it turns the cow's brain and spinal cord into a spongy-type matter. Slowly, the cow's mental and physical health begin to deteriorate.

3. Mad cow disease is transmitted by cows eating the suspect protein. Since cows are often fed the remains of other cattle (something

yummy called meat and bone meal), it's easy for an entire herd to become infected at once if they share the same food source.

4. Mad cow disease ultimately leads to the infected cow's death. There is no cure.

In the United Kingdom, the country most affected, the disease had reached epidemic proportions. Because of its ability to spread to both cattle and humans, over four million cattle were killed as a precaution.

Now, if humans were to contract mad cow disease through infected meat, they would share the same fate as the cows. Neurological functions would begin to slow down, causing psychosis, uncontrollable body movements, and eventually coma and death.

What struck me about mad cow disease was its similarity to the phenomenon of burnout in the church. (Don't ask me *how* my brain made that leap. All I know is that it did, and here we are!) We'll explore the similarities below.

WHAT YOU CAN'T SEE CAN HURT YOU

Characteristic: The disease lies dormant for a given amount of time, going unnoticed. It can be a period of months to a few years before the disease is found.

The first characteristic, the fact that the disease is unnoticed for a period of time, couldn't be truer in the context of burnout.

Remember the job I accepted in student ministry?

The church was in a rapidly growing community, and my new job couldn't have been better. Our team chemistry was nothing short of amazing. The momentum grew, the number of kids whose lives were changed grew, our staff grew—and everything was healthy and thriving. Soon our one weekly service became two, we started planning our own camps and mission trips, and eventually my husband, Chris, joined the staff as a part-time worship leader.

Things were going so well. We were on top of the world. It seemed too good to be true.

And it was.

Because I loved my job so much, I (proudly) didn't take a single vacation day during my first year on staff. By the end of our summer camp (which I was responsible to manage), I was exhausted.

Needless to say, the quickness of the onset of my weariness caught me off guard. The job I had once looked forward to tackling every single workday (and sometimes on my days off) I was now dreading.

Since I had allowed spending time with God to be replaced by spending time doing things *for* God, my spiritual tank had been sucked dry. When that happened, I began to lose perspective on almost every area of my life. My defenses were down, and I allowed myself to start believing the little lies the enemy would throw into my path.

> *You know, they are totally taking advantage of you. With your experience in management, they should be paying you double what you're making.*
>
> *Do you really think what you're doing matters? You're just a little girl on the support staff. Nobody really cares what you think. You'll never be able to lead like one of the guys. It's just the world you're in.*
>
> *And all that stuff you see and hear in staff meetings? You know this place is nothing but egos and trouble.*
>
> *Come on. You know you shouldn't be working in this church world. You shouldn't even be in a church. Life was so much better when you could pretend these things didn't exist.*

The smart thing at this point would have been to talk to somebody about what I was going through, but ministry was supposed to be so professional — so perfect.

I kept quiet.

As these thoughts were allowed to simmer silently over the course of a few weeks, I became more convinced these voices were right, so I started looking for a job back in the marketplace. Back where it didn't matter what your gender or your age was. If you put in the time, had the ideas, and made it to happy hour, you'd have all the respect you need to make it to the top.

However, when my efforts proved fruitless, I was discouraged. I actually began feeling guilty about working at the church, since there were so many people who would kill for the chance to be in vocational ministry.

Then out of left field, our church's administrator and senior pastor approached me about a new position that had been created — director of communication and media.

Director? The word seemed to shimmer and glimmer with prestige and power.

This new position would allow me to use my marketing and communications background. I'd oversee all areas of communication and media for the weekend services. I'd get to manage two creative teams. I'd get my own office. I'd be the youngest person on our leadership staff.

Director. Director. *Director!* Man. That sure had a nice ring to it!

I was in. This had to be the answer! I told our youth pastor I was going to be changing positions. He asked me to reconsider and told me I was probably letting the exhaustion of our intense summer schedule get the best of me. Deep down, I think I knew he was right, but I was dead set on taking the new position. So after helping with the transition of bringing in a new hire to our student staff, I moved over to the administration offices, high and lofty, on the second floor of a bank building. I'd be rubbing elbows with our senior leadership staff every day.

This was it! This was the good life.

Like most new things, every aspect of my new position was perfect. My strengths in problem solving and management were being put to good use, as both the communication and media areas were a mess. I was asked to help brand the church, redo the website, strengthen our weekend experiences, and involve and equip new volunteers.

I thought things were intense in student ministry, but the new position made my old schedule look like a summer vacation. Because our church was literally bursting at the seams, we had services on Saturday nights and all day on Sundays. We also had an off-site venue with multiple service times. My scheduled day off was Friday, but I'd often find myself finalizing weekend logistics on Friday afternoon and evening.

It was the only way to get it done. And, hey — it was all "for God." I believed thousands of people were relying on *my* talent every weekend to help engage them in their worship experience. Everything had to be perfect. I would settle for nothing less.

And as time went by, I was still none the wiser to the fact that my pride and I were continuing on a downward spiral.

My busy schedule also provided me a break from the tensions Chris and I were experiencing at home. I chalked it up to us still being newlyweds in an adjustment period, but whatever it was — I wanted away.

Our relationship during those first couple of years was nothing more than surface. I talked a big game — how marriage was a priority. We signed up for all the right couples classes and got involved in a small group for married people. We held hands and went to services and church events with big smiles on our faces.

We talked about my schedule constantly, and I'd always promise to do a better job of taking time off. But I never kept those promises. He warned me if I kept burning the candle at both ends, I would eventually burn out.

I refused to believe him.

And he was right.

About six months into my new position, I started feeling some tightness in my chest and had difficulty breathing. My doctor sent me to an allergy and asthma doctor, who in turn discovered I had pretty severe acid reflux. He scheduled an esophagogastroduodenoscopy (also known as an EGD), which is pretty much a fancy way of saying, "You get to swallow a camera so we can make sure your esophagus hasn't disintegrated."

The test was over quickly and found nothing too remarkable — just some minor inflammation that could easily be healed. They told me that if I experienced any stomach pain or peculiar symptoms for the next day or so, I should come back, as there was a slight risk they could have punctured my stomach during the procedure.

Hmmm. That's nice to know.

Expecting nothing out of the ordinary, I hung out at home on my day off. Somewhere around noon, I went from very normal to very sick — very quickly.

I drove myself back to the hospital where they had performed the procedure. They quickly admitted me to the ER and did some blood work and a CT scan. Chris had just arrived when the doctor came in.

"We think you might have appendicitis, but we're not sure. The CT showed you have abdominal inflammation, but your blood work is fine. To be safe, we're going to admit you, start you on some antibiotics, and watch you for a while."

Appendicitis isn't the end of the world. I was a little freaked out about the possibility of having surgery (and probably more freaked out that I'd have to miss work unexpectedly), but I was relieved I wasn't bleeding internally. They gave me some medicine for my pain and scheduled some tests for the next day.

One day of tests led to two. Two quickly became five. Each day it seemed my pain increased. And after every test, the doctor would come in and say the same thing.

"Well, we still haven't found a cause for your inflammation and pain. So tomorrow, we're going to do more tests."

I thought I'd never get out of the hospital.

After a week, and after what seemed like every test they could run had been performed, a couple of the doctors came in with some theories as to my ailment. One of them asked how my stress level was.

Chris accidentally let a little snort of laughter slip out.

That wasn't the best thing he could have done. I quickly shot him the evil eye.

Turning back to the doctors, I explained my schedule and the demands of my position at the church, justifying it with the fact I was only twenty-five and really in perfect health. A little stress never killed anyone.

And then one of the doctors explained to me that if I didn't change my lifestyle, I'd probably be back in the hospital within the year.

UNHEALTHY FROM ALL ANGLES

Characteristic: Mad cow disease is caused by a mutated protein that attaches itself to the cow's central nervous system, thus affecting the cow's brain and responses (hence the name). Essentially, it turns the cow's brain and spinal cord into a spongy-type matter. Slowly, the cow's mental and physical health begin to deteriorate.

Another interesting element to mad cow disease is the way in which it affects all areas of the cow's health. The cows begin suffering both physical and mental symptoms. They begin to lose their ability in muscle coordination, and in the most advanced stages they deteriorate socially, isolating themselves from their herd. Cows begin to display abnormal behaviors, including aggression and fear.

Unlike our bovine friends, we have an additional area that makes up our health. We share the physical, mental, and social (what I'll call relational) aspects with the cows, but we also have *spiritual health* to take into consideration. Even though these areas do affect us in their own unique ways, they also overlap into each other (*see illustration on next page*).

At the time, it was obvious that my physical health was suffering. As I laid for days in a hospital bed, cocktails of medicines being injected into my bloodstream, I couldn't help but wonder what damage my decisions had caused in other areas. Obviously the damage that had accumulated over the last three years had also affected my heart — one thing God wants completely.

After my trip to the hospital, my body was undergoing healing, but the other areas of my health continued to decline. Even though I was becoming stronger physically, the deepest sense of who I was had wilted away so slowly, I didn't even realize it.

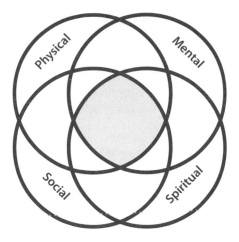

My emotional health probably suffered the most noticeable damage. I had never really dealt with long bouts of excessive worry before, but during this period, worry consumed me. I was anxious about my health, anxious because I knew I was dropping the ball, anxious that something bad would happen to Chris, anxious that someone would break into our house, anxious to drive, anxious that I would have a meltdown — and that's just the start!

Because of all the worry, I began losing sleep (which only made matters worse). Relationally, I began withdrawing from friendships and accountability because I didn't want anyone to think I was weak for struggling with so many things. I always needed to be the strong one. The dependable one. The rock. It was the only way I thought I could make it in ministry.

The lack of personal interaction, along with my fear and lack of sleep, put me into a depression. Even getting out of bed was a chore, and some days I didn't make it.

My relationship with God during this time was desperate but unfocused. Still believing the lie that I could save the world by myself, I didn't know what to pray for. I felt like a failure as a Christ-follower because I couldn't keep my act together enough to make a difference in the world — which was the cry of my heart.

One of our associate pastors—a good friend—noticed the confusion I was wearing on my sleeve once I returned to the office after my hospital stay. He came into my office, and we talked about the things I had experienced.

As important as my physical wake-up call was, it was nothing compared to the impact of the question he asked me: "Does working at this church interfere with your communion with Christ?"

I sat in my chair, stunned. With nothing left to do but say what both of us were thinking, I replied, "Yes."

But how could it? How could working in a church with an amazing staff, serving a wonderful community, *all for God*, interfere with my own relationship with my Father?

I didn't have the answer. But I knew, beyond a shadow of a doubt, that I was so wrapped up in doing, I had forgotten how to simply be.

How to be a child to a Father

How to be a vessel he can use

How to be a wife to my husband

How to be a light in a dark world

My friend's question haunted me for weeks.

CONTAMINATION

> *Characteristic: Mad cow disease is transmitted by cows eating the suspect protein. Since cows are often fed the remains of other cattle (something yummy called meat and bone meal), it's easy for an entire herd to become infected at once if they share the same food source.*

I always thought cows ate grass. Evidently, this isn't always the case. In Europe, where mad cow disease was first discovered, cows were being fed a sheep by-product meal mixed with their grain. The meal contained a mutated sheep protein called *prion*, which, when ingested, changes into a harmful agent and infects the cow with the disease. In the 1990s, when the outbreak of mad cow disease spread throughout the United Kingdom, it was the result of the cattle industry beginning to feed rendered, prion-infected bovine meat and bone meal to young calves.[1]

It's pretty gross, but cows became infected with the disease by eating the by-products of other infected cattle.

In both positions I had at the church, I know that my unhealthy attitude affected those around me. I worked closely with other staff and dozens of volunteers and projected my high expectations on them. If I gave up my nights and weekends, I assumed they would do the same. There was almost an unhealthy competitiveness in my spirit. If my boss came in early, I had to be there earlier. If she stayed late, I'd wait until after she'd leave to go home.

Oh, and I wanted to prove that I loved Jesus more.

At least, that was what I believed.

I thought the more I sacrificed, the more I loved Jesus. The more hours I put in for God's work, the more I was committed to his cause. I wanted to make my God proud, and I did a great job at it.

The only problem? God wasn't my God. My pride was my god.

Sometimes our environments contribute to the expectations we have as volunteers, as family members, or as church staff members.

The fear of letting people down, especially in spiritual matters, can often cause us to feel obligated or pressured into meeting unrealistic expectations, or worse, spending more time doing things *for* God instead of being what God wants us to be. That can lead to serious stress.

What's worse, it's easy for the resulting attitudes to contaminate a team or even an entire church.

Nothing will inhibit the Spirit from working in the church (as in all of us, not just *your* church) faster than bitterness. Than anger. Than pride. Than envy. Than laziness. Than lust. Than gossip. All of these things are deeply rooted issues that can spread and contaminate an entire body.

We become sick.

When we're sick, how can we show a dying world health? When we're hopeless, how can we show hope?

We can't.

SOMEONE'S OUT TO DESTROY YOU

> *Characteristic: Mad cow disease ultimately leads to the infected cow's death. There is no cure.*

I can imagine Satan hanging out in a recliner with his feet propped up, thinking what a fantastic job he did stealing, killing, and destroying me during that very hard season in my life. Slowly and subtly, my defenses weakened and I allowed myself to be taken down. And not only did he take *me* down; the decisions I made affected my husband, my coworkers, my friends, and my church family.

Mad church disease can and will strip away everything from your identity — from who you are in Christ. Why? Because the chief bearer of the disease only *wants* to destroy you.

John in his gospel records what Jesus said to a crowd of listeners:

"The thief comes only to steal and kill and destroy" (John 10:10a).

I realize this is a verse you are probably very familiar with — but that fact doesn't make it any less true. And I'd like to point out one word: "The thief comes *only* to steal and kill and destroy" (emphasis mine).

Only.

> *Only.*

> > *ONLY!*

The one objective the enemy has is to steal, kill, and destroy you. You may have heard somebody say, "If you're doing really good work for the Lord, Satan's going to try to stop you," or, "When you're really a threat to the devil, that's when he'll attack the hardest."

I don't think there is an "if" or a "when" about it. Satan is out to destroy you *no matter what!*

And if Satan can put things in your path to trip you up and take others down with you, I'm sure there's no better way he'd rather spend his time. He's going to ask himself how he can kill as many birds with one stone as possible. When the death and destruction of Christ-followers is the main goal, the enemy is going to think strategically.

Cows don't have much hope when they are infected with mad cow disease. Even though the process can take years, they die. There's no vaccine. We're a bit more fortunate. Satan's sole purpose in life is to ruin us — but God's sole purpose in life is to redeem us.

Cows don't get a second chance — but we are promised a second chance, and more.

The rest of Jesus' statement in John 10:10 reads,

"I have come that they may have life, and have it to the full."

And that's the amazing thing about grace. Regardless of how we struggle or how we fall, regardless of how many people are affected by our actions, God is a God of healing. God is a God of restoration and life.

Satan loves to steal and destroy what God has intended for good. He wants us to kill our ministry, our passion, and our hope so that we're useless. Through Christ, we're made complete. It's time to truly realize that — and begin to claim back what is rightfully ours.

⊕ EXAM ROOM

Where are you on your journey right now? Are you wondering how anyone can possibly burn out with such an amazing call on their life? Or have you seen it all, and maybe now you've hit rock bottom?

Do you have people in your life with whom you can openly share?

Satan comes only to steal, kill, and destroy. What areas in your life are most vulnerable? Jot them down here, and pray that God will continue to show you how to protect them.

Second Opinion

Bill Hybels, senior pastor, Willow Creek Community Church, South Barrington, Illinois

A. J.: You've mentioned that you've come close to being sidelined from ministry a couple of times. What led you to that place, and how did you recognize that what you were experiencing was endangering what you refer to as your "holy discontent"?

B. H.: On two occasions I allowed the growth of our church and the growth of the international component of what we do to lead to a level of stress that became unhealthy. It didn't quench my passion for the local church; I just realized that I was going to have to pace myself differently, organize the staff and my colleagues for more effective service, and change internal structures and procedures so that I could continue to pursue my God-given passions in a healthy way as opposed to getting overly exhausted or psychologically worn down.

A. J.: What boundaries did you set up in your life, both personally and professionally, that helped to keep you from moving into a self-reliant mode?

B. H.: I'm a firm believer in the spiritual disciplines. For example, I'm very committed to a pattern of solitude — secret acts of service, prayer, and journaling. I try to engage in daily journaling to chronicle the activity of God in my life and to help me sort out the complexities and the distractions that always seem to crop up. I'm also quite disciplined with my workday. I leave the office between 4:00 and 4:30 almost every single day. I watch how many nights in a row I'm out in a given ministry week. I take Sunday afternoons and Mondays off every single week, and in the summertime, I take a summer study break to allow a physical and emotional and spiritual "refilling" of sorts to counterbalance the "output" mode that typically characterizes my life.

A. J.: Once someone identifies his or her "holy discontent" — such as serving the poor or eradicating treatable diseases or helping people repair tenuous marriages or enfolding wounded people into community — it's easy for them to care so much about that particular firestorm-of-frustration issue that they unintentionally fall into a pattern of obsessive thoughts and behaviors in their noble attempt to join God in his kingdom-building activity. Sometimes exhaustion even sets in. What advice do you have for church leaders and their families for pursuing their areas of holy discontent in God-honoring ways?

B. H.: I like to look at that whole subject matter holistically. To engage in a cycle of working incredibly hard and then resting up is to rejuvenate only partially. There must also be consideration given to what you're reading, who you're surrounding yourself with, and what recreational activities you're pursuing that will genuinely refill your tanks. Especially as leaders in the church, we consistently need to be filled up and buoyed in our spirits because everybody takes their cue from the leader. If the leader is exhausted, then the people following that leader will feel exhausted. If the leader is wearing thin on hope, then people start losing hope too. If the leader gets pessimistic, everybody gets pessimistic. You see where this is going.

A. J.: What are some of the diseases you see plaguing the church today?

B. H.: I see twin towers of concern. One is burnout; the other is complacency. There are a lot of Christ-followers who haven't taken the time to figure out what their holy discontent is, and so they're doing a gradual slide into apathy and complacency — and that is unconscionable in a broken and lost world. I'm as concerned about Christ-followers' apathy as I am about other believers who are borderline exhausted. I would hope we could find the kind of energy that comes only from the Holy Spirit so that we can sustain productive, Christ-honoring ministry over the long haul.

CHAPTER 2

THE
EMERGENCY

When the notion of writing this book first struck me, I did a little bit of research. A couple of things surprised me.

First, there aren't very many books or readily available resources dealing with burnout in ministry. An online book search gave me a handful of results when I looked for the words "Church" and "Burnout" in titles. Out of that small number, only a couple of the books were still in print. That led me to wonder if there was even a need for discussion of this topic. Maybe the lack of books and resources meant a lack of interest.

I decided to probe a bit further and created an anonymous, online questionnaire to see what people were thinking about burnout—if they were thinking anything at all. Since I knew that burnout didn't just affect people on church staffs but families and volunteers as well, questions were developed for all three groups.

In July 2007, the website madchurchdisease.com was launched, and with the help of a viral Web 2.0 campaign, within just a couple of days almost a thousand people had taken the surveys. My email account was actually shut down by my provider due to the increased number of emails I was receiving and sending. They thought I was a spammer! Multitudes of people were sharing their stories, their struggles with working in ministry, and their feelings about it all—feelings they thought they could never share with anyone.

And the second thing that surprised me? A resounding voice was crying out, "I am burned-out! And evidently I'm not alone. I thought I was the only one."

Now these surveys weren't scientific in any way, but they did capture a snapshot of what a number of people involved in ministry were experiencing and provide some noteworthy demographics.

NOTEWORTHY QUESTIONNAIRE RESULTS

Location: As we looked at the responses, the locations of people who responded to the questionnaires proved interesting. Although most were from the United States, people from every continent but Antarctica participated. There were pastors from Peru, volunteers from New Zealand, wives of pastors from Scotland, staff leaders in Malaysia and Egypt and Turkey and Hong Kong. And that's just the tip of the iceberg.

Age: Another interesting finding was the ages of people who answered questions. We were assuming that a majority of responses would come from Gen X and Gen Y, yet surprisingly many people in their fifties — even sixties and seventies — completed the questionnaire.

Position in leadership: The people who were interested in the concept of mad church disease weren't just pastors. Besides spouses, children, or siblings of those in ministry, practically any position you could dream up in a church was represented. Pastors of all kinds, from lead pastors to worship pastors to children's pastors — as well as those holding a variety of support staff roles and creative roles, even those with the all-encompassing title of "worker bee" — showed they had experienced burnout or knew of someone who had.

Length of time in ministry: Another nondiscriminating factor for ministry burnout is the length of time spent in ministry. From just a few weeks in ministry to almost forty years, the ministry span of those affected by mad church disease is vast.

Accountability: Most people who responded to the survey had some kind of accountability in place, such as an accountability partner. Many people desire to have that person in their life; however, most people indicated they had, at some point in time, lied to that person.

Tangible effects: Almost every person who completed the questionnaire said the stress from ministry had affected them either emotionally (most common were feelings of worthlessness, depression, anxiety, anger, or loneliness) or physically (most common problems were insomnia, headaches, stomach problems, heart issues, weight gain, or inflammation).

Bible study: When asked about spending time in Bible study, apart from "studying for sermons or teaching," a quarter of those who responded said they didn't.

MOVING ON TO SCIENTIFIC RESEARCH

Realizing that my online questionnaire wasn't scientific and was a bit biased, I continued researching to see if there was any scientific data that would confirm the prevalence of burnout symptoms in the church.

Ellison Research, a research firm located in Phoenix, Arizona, has conducted several studies of the health of ministers and ministers' families.[1] These studies, conducted from 2002 to 2005 in all fifty states of the United States, spanned all Protestant denominations and sizes. I was excited to see if their scientific research would confirm my own findings and feelings.

Physical Health

When my husband and I got married in 2003, both of us were right around our ideal weight for our height. We had also started working in ministry that year. Now, I'm not saying that the two are entirely related, or that ministry "made" us gain weight, but because we didn't manage our schedules and plan our meals well, over the course of the next three to four years, we each gained thirty to forty pounds! Realizing the damage this was causing us, we both took steps to lose the weight we had gained. We're now back down to healthy weights, but we know if we're not careful, we could quickly pack on the pounds and harm our bodies by what we consume.

Insomnia and other sleep issues are also prevalent in the culture and within the church. According to a 2003 study, sleep deprivation costs $150 billion each year in higher stress and reduced worker productivity.[2]

Physical health is not a topic the Bible shies away from. David in Psalm 139 writes of our bodies as being fearfully and wonderfully created by God. I like the cut-and-dried approach Paul takes in 1 Corinthians 6:20: "You were bought at a price. Therefore honor God with your body."

It's easy to neglect our physical health when we're faced with the demands of ministry — whether it's our vocation or whether we've chosen to volunteer. Unfortunately, many of us take our health for granted.

The 568 senior pastors surveyed by Ellison Research were described as "not in terribly good shape physically." Collectively, they averaged less than seven hours of sleep per night, were more than thirty pounds overweight, and maintained poor eating habits.[3]

BREAKDOWN – SCIENTIFIC PROOF: PHYSICAL HEALTH OF PASTORS

EATING HABITS/WEIGHT ISSUES

- 71 percent of all ministers admitted to being overweight by an average of 32.1 pounds. One-third of all ministers were overweight by at least 25 pounds, including 15 percent who were overweight by 50 pounds or more.
- Two-thirds of all pastors skip a meal at least one day a week, and 39 percent skip meals three or more days a week.
- 83 percent eat food once a week that they know they shouldn't because it is unhealthy, including 41 percent who do this three or more days a week.
  88 percent eat fast food at least one day a week, and 33 percent eat fast food three or more days a week.
- 50 percent get the recommended minimum amount of exercise (30 minutes per day, three times a week); 28 percent don't exercise at all.

STRESS-RELATED HEALTH ISSUES

- Four out of ten ministers (approximately 39 percent)

reported digestive problems once a week, with 14 percent having chronic digestive problems (three days per week).

- 87 percent don't get enough sleep at least once a week, with almost half (47 percent) getting less sleep than they need at least three nights a week. Only 16 percent regularly get the recommendation of eight hours or more per night.
- 52 percent experience physical symptoms of stress at least once a week, and nearly one out of four experiences physical symptoms three or more times a week.

Ron Sellers, president of Ellison Research, says the youngest ministers seem to have the unhealthiest lifestyles:

The youngest ministers are the heaviest, the most likely to skip meals, the most likely to eat unhealthy foods, the least likely to get exercise, the most likely to go without sufficient sleep, the least likely to take vitamins, the most likely to eat fast food, and the most likely to report problems sleeping. It might be argued that these are eager young ministers out trying to change the world, or at least to build their careers. But it's tragic that they apparently are sacrificing their own health for these purposes.[4]

Health of the Pastor's Family

If you are a family member of a pastor or church staff member, you know only too well the extra pressure that comes with being in the ministry — the high expectations placed on him or her and the hours spent away from the family.

I have several friends who are children of pastors or church staff members. Among them is Ruth, the daughter of a music minister. When she and her sister were in junior high and high school, they formed a group called "The Ministers' Kids Support Group for Psychiatric Help," complete with a constitution, pledge, and actual support group meetings. They invited other pastors' children to it. It was partially a joke, she tells me, but partially not. The pledge began with, *"I am a minister's kid. There is absolutely nothing I can do about it!"*

Craig Groeschel, senior pastor at LifeChurch.tv, wrote about a lesson he learned from his daughter Catie early in his ministry.

When my first daughter, Catie, was very young, I was the classic overly-driven, ministry-obsessed, type-A personality workaholic. While working full-time as an associate pastor, I was also carrying fifteen hours of seminary classes.

One day I called little Catie on the phone and said I had to stay late at the office to get some work done and would not see her before she went to bed. I promised her I would be home and wake her with a late good night kiss.

Catie innocently said, "Daddy, this is not your home. You live at the office."

I changed my work habits at that moment and have never been the same.[5]

BREAKDOWN – SCIENTIFIC PROOF: HEALTH OF THE PASTOR'S FAMILY

FAMILY HEALTH: SELF

- 94 percent agree with the statement, "There is extra pressure being married to a minister," including 54 percent who strongly agree.
- 91 percent agree there is extra pressure being the child of a pastor; 46 percent strongly agree.
- Six out of ten pastors say that their role as a minister prevents them from spending sufficient time with their family.
- On a scale of 1 (extremely unhealthy) to 5 (extremely healthy), pastors were asked to rate the health of their family relationships. The average rating for their relationship with their spouse was 4.5 out of 5, with 47 percent considering their relationship extremely healthy.
- Overall, pastors rated their family health as a 4.

FAMILY HEALTH: VIEW OF OTHER PASTORS

- Although pastors give their family relationships high marks (4), when asked to rate the health of other pastors' families, the average rating was 3.2.
- The average minister estimates that 25 percent of pastors he or she knows are having relational issues with a child, and 20 percent of other pastors are having considerable problems in their marriage.

Ellison Research's president Ron Sellers noted the difference between how pastors see their own family health and how they see the health of other clergy families. "Ministers apparently have a much more optimistic view of their own family than they do of the families of other ministers," Sellers stated. "When one out of every twenty ministers feels his or her own family unit is unhealthy, but one out of every seven ministers believes the family units of others in their denomination are unhealthy, there's a disconnect."

Sellers added, "One of these perspectives probably is wrong—either things are not as bad with other ministers' families as the typical pastor believes, or things are not as healthy with their own family as the typical pastor believes."[6]

Based on this research, even if only 5 percent of pastors are in seriously unhealthy relationships with their families, that's almost 20,000 people. And that is just an estimate of senior pastors; it doesn't include other church staff workers or volunteers.

PASTORS' SATISFACTION WITH PRAYER LIFE

Have you ever read a book that totally wrecked you? For me that book was *Preacher and Prayer* by E. M. Bounds.[7]

In *Preacher and Prayer*, Bounds describes the prayer habits of several Christian men — and not just vocational pastors.

- John Wesley prayed for two hours every morning, starting at 4:00 a.m.

- Edward Payson prayed so often that deep grooves were formed on his hardwood floor by his bedside from where he knelt.

- Abolitionist William Wilberforce spent at least two hours in prayer early in the day.

- John Welch, a Scottish preacher, would think he wasted his day if he spent less than eight to ten hours a day in prayer, sometimes in the middle of the night.

When I first read about these men, I was blown away. To be honest, for me prayer has usually been an afterthought. Or I'd pray when people would request something specific, but I don't think I've ever prayed for probably more than half an hour at a time. And certainly not at 4:00 a.m.! My prayer life was lacking depth. And evidently mine wasn't the only one.

BREAKDOWN – SCIENTIFIC PROOF: SATISFACTION OF PRAYER LIFE

- The average pastor prays 39 minutes a day.
- 21 percent of pastors pray less than 15 minutes a day.
- Those most satisfied with their prayer life spend almost an hour in prayer per day; those who are least satisfied with their prayer life average 21 minutes per day.
- Those most satisfied spend less time making requests and more time being quiet and listening to God; those least satisfied spend a majority of their prayer time making requests.[8]

I realize it's not how long or when you pray that's important. But what was consistent with these men mentioned by Bounds, as well as with several biblical examples — Jacob, David, Daniel, Paul, Jesus — was the *sacrifice* of their own desires (such as sleep or convenience).

Bounds writes,

> What the church needs today is not more machinery or better, not
> new organizations or more and novel methods, but men whom
> the Holy Ghost can use — men of prayer, men mighty in prayer.
> The Holy Ghost does not flow through methods, but through men.
> He does not come on machinery, but on men. He does not anoint
> plans, but men — men of prayer.[9]

With prayer being one of the cornerstones of our spiritual disciplines
and essential for communion with our Father, it's surprising that such a
high number of ministers are not satisfied with their prayer lives.

CASUALTIES OF WAR

It's obvious in the arena of pastors and church leaders that there's a
classic battle going on between good and evil. We know what we need
to do — to take care of our bodies, our minds, our souls, and our families — but we allow the idol of convenience to replace the knowledge
that the Holy Spirit has instilled in us.

Biological warfare has been around for a very long time, but the threats
have moved up in our consciousness after September 11, 2001. Terror-
ists can release lethal biological agents in a small confined space, and
because of their careful planning and knowledge of the agent and their
target, incurable disease and destruction will rapidly follow.

Satan works in a similar manner. He's been plotting since the fall to
ruin mankind, and what better place to start than with the one group
of people whose purpose it is to share life with a hurting world. All
it takes is infecting one person, and the epidemic can spread like
wildfire.

If I were a betting girl, I'd place my money on the fact that almost everyone reading this book has had some type of encounter with a pastor
or church leader who has fallen victim to one of the "big three" — sex,
money, or power. Almost everybody struggles significantly in at least
one of these three areas.

And in worst-case scenarios, you've seen how this person's public struggles have affected more than just the person himself or herself.

My good friend Allen was the lead pastor of a healthy suburban church. For over a dozen years, he had led the church to catch an incredible vision of reaching their local community for Christ. The church had consistently grown for almost twenty years, from about 150 to around 5,000, and had relocated numerous times, most recently into a newly constructed building near several cookie-cutter subdivisions in which working-class dads and soccer moms had taken up residence.

Allen's passion was unquenchable. His heart, worn on his sleeve, was inspiring for anyone who spent time with him. Kimberly, his beautiful wife and mother to his kids, was always seen around the church — involved in the choir, mothers programs, and Bible studies for women.

Allen's "big three" struggle? Sex.

Please don't misunderstand me. I realize we *all* have our struggles — areas in which Satan tends to home in on with laserlike precision. And no one sin is greater than another. However, with the knowledge of your weaknesses comes the responsibility to protect these areas with the greatest amount of armor possible.

This was the misfortune in Allen's situation. Since he was ashamed of his weakness, he didn't share it with anyone, not even with those who held him accountable. Because Allen believed the lie that nobody would understand his struggle, he also began believing other lies — that he was falling in love with another woman, for example.

The constant demands wore down his sense of worth, and with the growth the church was experiencing, more and more people needed to be pleased. After spending hours and hours pouring his life into ministry, doing the work that comes with leading a church, Allen slowly began to drop his guard.

The relationship with the other woman was an escape. What he knew was wrong became twisted into what was right. And he couldn't stop. The on again/off again extramarital affair lasted for years, until one day it couldn't go on anymore. He couldn't lead the church, and he knew it. He was too afraid of being found out. So Allen suddenly tendered his resignation.

God had other plans.

The elder board met with him, asking him to reconsider his position. They told him that if he was stressed-out because of all the new growth, new bills, and new people, they'd give him as much time off as he needed. Allen knew that this wasn't the case. After meeting with the elders for several hours, he confessed.

The elders and leadership team immediately met with church staff members and told them the sad news. Key volunteers were also notified. And the decision was made to announce the resignation to the congregation the following Sunday.

Because of this pastor's prominence in his community, the news hit with the impact of nothing short of a tidal wave. As one of the other pastors read a letter to the church, gasps of shock and sounds of weeping were heard throughout the room. And of course, bad news travels fast. It seemed as though the whole metropolitan area knew before the day was over what had happened, and sadly, most of what was being passed along was simply exaggerated gossip.

People began discussing the situation online. Because of the story's trauma, even those who were unfamiliar with the church and the pastor kept spreading the word. What had first affected just one man now affected thousands of people in one community. And then it turned into epidemic proportions, affecting tens — possibly hundreds — of thousands of people around the world.

A friend of mine spoke with Allen a few days after he had resigned. If his voice was any indication of his soul, Allen's was totally shattered. My friend said that if his and Allen's conversation had been recorded and then mailed to believers everywhere, people would never have affairs again.

Allen was *that* broken.

Although Allen fell out of God's will, he didn't fall out of God's reach. Allen faced a seemingly impossible restoration. It would take a miracle.

In spite of the terrible pain his decisions caused him, his family, and thousands of people, God picked Allen up, dusted him off, and said, "OK. Now how can we use this for my glory?"

God does the same with us every single day. Seven months into his healing, Allen told me, "There's no doubt I have to live with the consequences. There's no doubt I have a long, long way to go. But grace has never been so real to me. I could preach about grace all day long, but I had never truly experienced it until now."

In Allen's case, there is no doubt that God has his work cut out for him. But isn't that true for all of us?

CODE BLUE

When a Code Blue is issued in a hospital, any available medical personnel run to the room of the person who is coding. It's a matter of life and death. Milliseconds count. Politics, personal beliefs, hang-ups, grudges, and pride are put aside as the life of a fellow human lies in their hands. It's an emergency.

Since the beginning of time, mankind has been facing a life-and-death emergency. We are separated from our Creator. All he wants is for us to be reconciled to him. He sent his own flesh and blood down to earth to restore us. And we're to help guide others to that restoration.

The greatest commandments are what? To love God and to love our neighbors as we love ourselves. In most cases, I don't question our love for God. The passion and intensity with which we go about our lives are small indicators of our love. But we are guilty of not loving ourselves. The statistics

Difficulty is the very atmosphere of miracle – it is miracle in its first stage. If it's to be a great miracle, the condition is not difficulty, but impossibility.

– Lettie B. Cowman,
Streams in the Desert

don't lie. And even if they did, I'm sure you could conclude from your own experience that, quite frankly, we're pretty terrible at loving ourselves.

If we can't love ourselves, we can't love others in the way that God has designed us. We can care for others and can want the best for them, but to love them in the godliest way is impossible until we can obey this great commandment.

We are in the midst of a crisis that needs our full devotion of mind, body, and spirit.

In Mark 12:30, Jesus declares, "Love the Lord your God with all your heart and with all your soul and with all your mind and with all your strength."

Notice Jesus doesn't tell us to "love *others* with all your strength"; he says to "love the Lord your God." By loving God, we're faithful to his commandments. And when we're obedient, God will carry out his work through us. He will prepare us for battle in all areas.

Satan is out to annihilate hope and light, both in our world and in us, the body of Christ. He's well aware of the crisis of the human race, and he will do anything and everything in his power to obliterate our efforts.

As the church, we need to take a good, hard look around and ask ourselves if we are ready to fight. To fight for our own love relationship with God through Christ, and for the world around us as well.

God ... wants to work in and through you. Let Him. Yield to Him, and let this be the day when you shall begin to live in the power of the mighty Indwelling One.

—F. B. Meyer

⊕ EXAM ROOM

As you look at the surveys mentioned in this chapter, do you relate to any of the statistics? Write down the ones most relevant to you, and spend some time thinking about your own perspectives on these issues.

What's your biggest temptation? Is it one of the "big three," or is it something else? How do you protect your integrity in small ways to keep yourself from falling victim to temptation?

As you've seen in this chapter, you're not alone in whatever it is you're facing. The world is in a state of emergency, and Satan is out to destroy. Ask God to bring some of your ministry friends to mind. Pray for them, and then contact them to let them know that you're standing with them in this battle.

Second Opinion

Perry Noble, senior pastor, NewSpring Church, Anderson, South Carolina

A. J.: What are some things you do to help you recognize when you need a breather?

P. N.: One of the first things I do is *try* to listen to my body. Whenever I catch myself with that tired feeling for more than two or three days, I know that rest is *much* needed.

Also I try to pay attention to how tolerant I am of other people. If I find myself getting upset at even the most trivial thing, it's time to break away for a while.

And finally, when I begin to think, "I just can't do this anymore," or, "I really wish I didn't have to preach this weekend," then I know that being stressed and tired are the sources of that line of thinking, because thinking that way goes against the calling that Jesus has placed on my life.

A. J.: When you struggle with something negative that you're having a hard time shaking, where do you turn?

P. N.: I have to honestly say that this question is something I am continually wrestling with and struggling through.

First of all, I really do find comfort and encouragement in the Scriptures. Also I turn to the team I serve with. They are able to help me see that, though the situation seems to be enormous and out of control, it is actually all in God's hands.

A. J.: When a disease is contagious, it can spread quickly and infect others. How do you combat mad church disease in your church?

P. N.: One of the things I've always done is directly confront any blatant untruths that are being said about the ministry God has given us. I usually do it in a humorous way, and in doing so, I've actually given the people in our church both ammunition and permission to confront untruthful things in love.

A. J.: Cows don't have a chance when it comes to surviving mad cow disease. Thankfully for us, one of God's favorite things to do is to restore our relationship with him and with others. When things look hopeless and God seems far away, what are some truths you meditate on?

P. N.: I meditate on the fact that he has called me into ministry, that he is sovereign and is not surprised by anything, that Jesus Christ endured *way* more than I will ever endure and he never quit, and so I shouldn't either. I think about how I feel, and I think about what is real — and they are often two separate things. I think about how God has given me the Holy Spirit to guide me through all situations — and God promises us life.

PART 2

AM I AT RISK? EXAMINING RISK FACTORS AND SYMPTOMS

"**Y**ou have *got* to be kidding me," I said to my doctor. "I'm only twenty-seven. I'm totally healthy!"

I was at my annual physical — or better to say, my once-a-decade physical. I hadn't had a full workup with my family practitioner since I was sixteen.

He rolled back on his little stool and flipped through my chart.

"I really do think you should have an EKG, just to be on the safe side. There are heart problems on both sides of your family, and especially with what your dad's been through and the fact that you seem to overload yourself — well, I just think it'd be a good idea."

I couldn't argue. He had been our family doctor for well over a decade and knew that my dad had had quintuple bypass heart surgery three years prior. And he had seen me through all my stressful ups and downs.

I let the nurse apply a dozen or so little suction cups to my body and get a readout of my heart's rhythms.

"Well, it looks like everything's good," the nurse said, and my doctor confirmed it. I walked out of the exam room to a waiting room full of people twice my age, waiting to get their own tickers checked.

I felt ridiculous as I passed them. But at the same time, I secretly appreciated my doctor's initiative. He knew I could have a genetic predisposition for heart problems, and he wanted to make sure we were being proactive with my health.

In order to get a good understanding of mad church disease, we've got to take a look at our health from every angle, starting at the beginning. Are certain kinds of people more likely to experience burnout? Does burnout happen because of our environment?

Taking a look back at my doctor's decision to run an EKG, I can tell he looked at both internal and external factors. Internally, he knew I had a family history of heart issues. Externally, he knew I often overcommitted myself, which could lead to unnecessary strain on my heart. Those two facts alone are significant risk factors for developing heart problems, even at an early age.

In the same vein, both internal and external factors contribute to mad church disease.

CHAPTER 3

INTERNAL
RISK FACTORS

Certain internal factors can make us more at risk for becoming burned-out. Most of these are features we are born with. They reflect how God knit together the fibers of our being. And because they are fairly hard-wired, these characteristics aren't easily changed, and that is OK. We have to accept the fact that, although these may sometimes seem like limitations, they are the very things that make us unique.

PERSONALITY TYPE

Most of us are familiar with type A and type B personality descriptors.[1] Look at the table below. Which personality type do you lean toward? (You may have both type A and type B characteristics, but you probably have a clear view of your dominant personality type.)

Type A Characteristics	Type B Characteristics
Impatient / Time conscious	Patient
Concerned about status	Relaxed
Competitive	Easygoing
Aggressive	Creative
Incapable of relaxing	Imaginative
Easily able to multitask	Self-analytical
Shows workaholic tendencies	Often described as laid-back

The general assumption is that type A personalities tend to burn out easier than type B, but it's not always the case.

Dean was a really casual kind of guy. He pastored a church in a small community — and he preferred to. His gentle demeanor was a stunning reflection of Christ, and his patience seemed endless. Although he was a great communicator, it wasn't because he had a charismatic personality. When he spoke, you *had* to listen. Every word was well-thought-out and inspiring. Because of his creative and easygoing personality, he was always thinking of new ways to reach people for Christ. And he had no problem with relaxing. You could find him early on Saturday mornings fishing in a nearby river with other men from the neighborhood.

It's pretty obvious Dean was a classic type B. He wasn't concerned about status. He was laid-back and imaginative. But because of his patience and easygoing personality, he had a very difficult time saying no.

Dean's burnout began very slowly. A few church members would drop by the parsonage unannounced. He would show them in, serve coffee and dessert, and patiently listen to their problems. What started out with a couple of people stopping in a couple of times a month turned into several members stopping by multiple times a week.

Dean's strengths of being sensitive and friendly also became his weaknesses. Because he didn't know how to set boundaries, his approach began handicapping him. Soon Dean's bucket became empty. He no longer had the energy to minister to others in the way he knew was necessary. His growing ineffectiveness triggered a depression, and he eventually left the ministry.

Dean took time off. He relaxed. He didn't continually go a hundred miles an hour. Yet Dean still burned out.

On the flip side, Janelle is a type A. She's a busy mom and wife who also works part-time in health care. Her husband travels frequently, and her sons, ages seventeen and twelve, are active in school and church activities.

Janelle has never received a paycheck from her church, but she's there several times a week. She serves as the worship service producer, making sure everyone is in the correct place at the correct time. She participates in the creative team planning for all the services. If there's a broken piece between the original brainstorming session and the execution of the service, Janelle will be the first to step up and fix it.

Her driven personality is essential for her volunteer role. God has gifted her to be organized and strategic, as well as energetic and full of a "Let's go get 'em, tiger!" attitude.

After three years of dutiful, dedicated service, Janelle called the media pastor and quit out of the blue. It was right before the Christmas season — and with her oldest son due to graduate in a few months, the stress of volunteer service on top of family responsibilities was just too much. Soon, Janelle wasn't seen around the church at all. Even though the media pastor would occasionally call to check in, Janelle faded away. She had burned out.

Like Dean, because Janelle didn't know how to manage her strength as a type A personality, it eventually became her Achilles' heel and took her out of the game.

OUR HISTORY

Another internal influence for developing mad church disease is our past, which is as unique as our personality. Our family structures as children, our education, and our spiritual journeys have an effect on how we see our lives today and on how we plan our future. Deeply rooted trauma or habitual choices made over time make us more inclined to act in certain ways. We still make our own decisions, but our past is what makes us distinct.

Take Cindy, for example. Growing up, she always earned good grades in school. Her parents encouraged her to participate in extracurricular activities, so she played sports, participated in the Spanish club, and helped mentor other students.

What Cindy was unable to realize at the time was the power her parents' expectations had over her. As long as she stayed on the honor roll and kept her social calendar full, they were happy. However, once her grades dropped, they expressed their disappointment. She decided to limit some of her activities to focus on her studies, but her parents became frustrated that she wasn't performing at a level acceptable to them.

Fast-forward fifteen years. Cindy now works as the volunteer women's director in her church. She also serves in the children's ministry and occasionally sings in the choir. Her parents no longer have an active influence on her decision making, but their impact still rings loud and clear.

Growing up, Cindy lived in a constant state of fear. She was afraid that if her perfect balance of school and extracurricular activities unraveled, her parents would be right there to let her know. And now that she's active in her church, the same fear of disappointment controls her emotions and behaviors around the clock.

Instead of trying to appease her parents, she tries to appease her ministry leader. She often takes work home with her, staying connected to her phone and email at all times. If something comes up, she doesn't want to let the ball drop. She's afraid that if she unplugs for even a moment, she'll be letting her team down.

Maybe you didn't receive much affirmation growing up, so you run yourself ragged trying to please others and fill that gaping hole you carry around. Or maybe one of your parents left, which put you in a position of having to be responsible at a young age — and now you can't let it go as an adult. So you're taking responsibility for others to make things work right. Perhaps you were traumatized or abused, and the only way you can numb the pain is to fill your life with busyness.

As much as we may want to, we can never rid ourselves of our past — the good *or* the bad. And regardless of how normal or how terrible your past may have been, you've experienced it all for a reason. The successes, the failures, the joy, and the pain are all beautifully woven together to make you who you are at this moment.

We should look at our past as a gift and not a burden. And as such, we should steward it like any other gift we've been given. We need to be grateful for our unique circumstances, not resentful. Once we accept our God-given past, we can find out what about it makes us extraordinary. How can we channel a propensity toward responsibility — as in Cindy's case? How can we encourage others who have a past similar to ours?

By taking our focus off the dysfunctions of our past, and changing it to how God can work through us as he uses our life journey — our history, our present, and our future — we are less likely to burn out. Any time we become less and God becomes more, it's *his* power being perfected in us.

OUR HEALTH

Our physical health impacts our day-to-day living more than we may realize. From our sleep habits to the way we eat or even exercise, our health can influence our susceptibility to burn out.

When I lived in Dallas, I got to know a pastor named Joe. Just a few weeks after meeting him, while I was doing some communication consulting with his church, Joe fell off the face of the earth.

With nothing but a short email telling me he would be away from the church for a few months, he directed me to another staff member. I wondered what had happened to Joe. Several months later, he contacted me and told me that his leadership team had forced him to take two months off from ministry. He was on the brink of total exhaustion.

The symptoms manifested in several ways — mostly a mixture of physical and spiritual effects. And his physical stress, compounded by a seething anger, had gotten to a point where it nearly killed him.

One easy way you can be taken down fast is by simply not taking care of yourself. The areas in your health you neglect now *will* eventually catch up to you. In Joe's case, it took almost an entire decade of ignoring the warning signs. We're given one shot at taking care of our bodies, and it's our decision whether we'll take the information available to us to make wise choices. Or we can ignore it — and burn out.

OUR RELATIONSHIP WITH CHRIST

Last, but certainly most important, is the way in which we walk with Christ in our daily relationship with him. Are we walking in such a way that each and every step is guided by the Spirit, or are we finding things to do and asking God only to bless *our* efforts?

The biblical story of David shows the indescribable closeness that comes when we humbly seek God and rely on his power, as well as the tragedy that inevitably strikes when we stray.

From the moment David was anointed to be king of Israel in 1 Samuel 16, it was obvious to those around him that God was with him. When one of Saul's attendants suggested that they find a harpist to help relieve the distress an evil spirit was causing Saul, another servant suggested David: "I have seen a son of Jesse of Bethlehem who knows how to play the harp. He is a brave man and a warrior. He speaks well and is a fine-looking man. *And the LORD is with him*" (1 Samuel 16:18, emphasis mine).

Later, David reappears when Goliath and the Philistines are challenging the Israelites. Even though it didn't make sense that a young man should take on a nine-foot giant, Saul agrees to let David go, saying, "The LORD be with you" (1 Samuel 17:37).

When all David should have wanted to do was run, he stood his ground against Goliath:

> David said to the Philistine, "You come against me with sword and spear and javelin, but *I come against you in the name of the LORD Almighty*, the God of the armies of Israel, whom you have defied. This day *the LORD will hand you over to me*, and I'll strike you down and cut off your head. Today I will give the carcasses of the Philistine army to the birds of the air and the beasts of the earth, and the whole world will know that there is a God in Israel."
>
> — 1 Samuel 17:45 – 46 (emphasis mine)

David had no armor. He had his past. God had given him experience fighting lions and bears as a shepherd. And God had given David the confidence he needed to go out *"in the name of the LORD Almighty."* In verse 46, David expresses that he knows — beyond a shadow of a doubt — that God will hand over Goliath to him so that David can finish him off. David clearly says it's not because of his strength, or even his weapons, that Goliath will fall.

It is simply because of God.

David's belief that God would deliver on his promises was all he needed.

Not for one moment when faced with Goliath and the Philistines did David buckle under the pressure. He never ran from it. The Bible never says he was even afraid; in fact, it suggests just the opposite: "As the Philistine moved closer to attack him, David ran quickly toward the battle line to meet him" (1 Samuel 17:48).

David *ran quickly* toward the battle line.

There are certainly times in our spiritual journeys when we feel that same fresh passion. We feel reckless because we are walking (or running) completely in God's power.

After David became king of Israel, he received a message from God through the prophet Nathan, reminding him of God's faithfulness in the past and God's desire to make a covenant with him for the future.

Throughout David's reign as king, he goes to war many, many times. He wins battle after battle. He blesses the house of Saul. He rules over Israel. Needless to say, David's a pretty busy guy. And over the course of time, he slowly begins to stray from God's perfect plan.

In 2 Samuel 11, it's springtime. Instead of spending time standing in awe of the budding trees and listening to the harmonies of the singing birds, the kings in that era went off to war. David was no exception. Even though he personally stayed in Jerusalem, he sent out armies to destroy the Ammonites.

We all know the story. David sees the beautiful Bathsheba bathing. He wants her. He gets her. They even conceived a child together.

Big oops.

Remember how David earlier had run toward the battle line to defeat Goliath? I'm pretty sure he was running hard and fast the other way now to get out of this mess.

He tells lies. He deceives his men. He devises a plan. He orders Uriah (Bathsheba's husband) home and gets him drunk so he'll sleep with his wife. Maybe they could pass the pregnancy off as what happened as a result of that encounter.

But it didn't work. Uriah was so devoted to his army that he turns down the offer of "special privileges." He refuses to sleep with Bathsheba while his men are still out fighting.

I can see David pacing the floor wondering how to take care of this situation. The only possible solution he saw was to kill Uriah.

And that's what happened. David makes a plan and sets Uriah up to die on the battle line. Not only did Uriah die, but other men in his army were killed in the fight.

The people who influence us the most are not those who detain us with their continual talk, but those who live their lives like the stars in the sky and "the lilies of the field" — simply and unaffectedly. Those are the lives that mold and shape us.

If you want to be of use to God, maintain the proper relationship with Jesus Christ by staying focused on him, and he will make use of you every minute you live — yet you will be unaware, on the conscious level of your life, that you are being used of him.

—Oswald Chambers,
My Utmost for His Highest

David continues to cover up his tracks by telling more and more lies. And for the first time in the Bible's account of David's life, it no longer says that *the LORD was with him.*

Instead, 2 Samuel 11:27 tells us, "But the thing David had done displeased the LORD."

We all make mistakes. We all screw up. And it doesn't mean that God leaves us. David wasn't perfect before meeting Bathsheba. But we can learn several things from his story.

We have a choice of what we keep in front of us: We can either keep our eyes focused on what God can accomplish through his power in our lives or choose to focus on what I call "the dangerous distractions."

When we are walking in step with God and in his power, he places his favor on us. Others notice that God is working in and through us. We, on the other hand, are completely oblivious to the intensity with which God is using us.

However, when we focus on the dangerous distractions, God simply won't stand for it. He offers his forgiveness, his mercy, and hope, to be sure, but we must confess and fall back on his strength before we move forward on the journey he has laid out for each of us.

⊕ EXAM ROOM

What personality type are you? Type A or type B?

What one thing do you appreciate about your past that makes you who you are today?

What one thing in your past have you had a hard time facing?

On a scale of 1 to 10, rate your overall health (1 being extremely poor; 10 being extremely good).

1 · · · **5** · · · **10**

What areas of your health could be internal risk factors for burning out? Are you ignoring them?

Can you identify some dangerous distractions in your life? What are some things you see that are out of your reach and out of God's plan but nonetheless lure you to still desire them and pursue them?

EXTERNAL RISK FACTORS

Although many internal factors can predispose us to experience burnout, certain things within our environment — external factors, in other words — when not handled appropriately, can influence our decisions negatively.

TOOLS OF OUR TOOLS

When I first started working in ministry, I had your everyday, ordinary cell phone. It placed and received calls, and that was pretty much it. Over time, and by my own free will, I've upgraded to the superphone. It emails. It sends texts. It checks the score of the Dallas Mavericks games. It wakes me up at 5:30 every morning and let's me snooze twice for ten minutes at a time. It keeps my calendar and gives me directions.

Can I be honest?

For a while my phone owned my life.

I lost control.

This fact actually struck me one day in the shower. I was getting ready to go to one of our weekend services when I had an idea about a project at work. So, since my phone was already in the bathroom (you know, just in case someone needed me), I actually started sending emails and text messages from *the shower*!

We always make fun of people who talk on their phones in the bathroom, or how unsanitary it is for people to use them to text or email while they're, how shall we delicately say it, "taking care of business" — but I really think I crossed a sad, sad line when I couldn't wait for five minutes and felt like I needed to send those messages right then and there from the shower.

That is a lack of control.

I confessed my shower email-sending episode to my husband (and now to you — how embarrassing!) I mean, really. Some things need to be left sacred.

Technology is a powerful tool, but as Henry David Thoreau once wrote, "Men have become the tools of their tools." I recently spent some time in Africa with Compassion International. We visited several projects where even the most primitive forms of technology did not exist. If we weren't in a hotel or restaurant, more than likely our bathroom was a hole cut in the ground.

One of the visions of our time in Africa was to have the trip participants, who were all bloggers, document in video, photography, and words what we saw and felt. Fifteen different perspectives reaching fifteen different audiences, all for the common goal of releasing children from poverty in Jesus' name.

Before the trip, organizers carefully researched the hotels in Kampala, Uganda, where we would be staying, so that Internet access would be guaranteed and we'd be able to blog consistently from Uganda. However, things didn't go as planned.

Our Internet service, if it worked, was slow at best (it took me an hour once to upload four small photos). Many of our cell phones didn't have international plans, so calling our families back home was also out of the question. The first few days I felt phantom BlackBerry alerts until I remembered that my phone had no signal in the middle of Africa.

No phone connections and sporadic Internet use forced the fifteen of us to disconnect in a way that probably none of us had ever done before.

Honestly, I think most of us were frustrated for the first few days — mainly because we were unable to share what we were experiencing with our readers. What's more, the inability to connect with our families and friends back home made us feel even more disconnected.

It is difficult to unplug. Internet is relatively inexpensive, as are mobile phones that receive email. Our TVs and TiVos and iPods and satellite radios give us comfort and convenience, but when we rely on them so heavily, they also give us headaches and no time for solitude.

LACK OF CONTROL

I know from my own experience as a PK, as well as from my time spent in ministry, that we often feel as though we don't have a choice in what we do or don't do. How many times have you said, "If I don't take care of this, it's never going to get done"? We assume the pressure is on us (and it very well might be), and as a result, we slowly begin to lose control over our thinking, and then over our behavior.

Aside from our phone/email/text addictions, other things can make us feel out of control. Sometimes we don't get to choose what our tasks are, and we're stuck doing something we're not passionate about. Sometimes we're constrained by financial challenges or a lack of other resources. Maybe the hours we're required to work are out of our control and becoming a pressure in the life we have outside of the office.

PRESSURE TO BE THE BEST

We are creatures who need affirmation. And the spotlight seems to promise us everything we've ever wanted. Whether it's an actual spotlight on the platform in front of an adoring congregation or a more passive spotlight — perhaps you glow under the praise of a certain leader — it's natural to seek out opportunities in which we can shine and be at our best.

One of the problems I see plaguing unhealthy environments is *ego*. Ego can show itself as loud and abrasive, or as subtle and deceiving. Either way, it's the antithesis of the character of Christ.

Society today is competitive. We feel that our voices must be the loudest and carry the furthest in order to be heard and validated. It breaks my heart when I hear pastors of small churches say, "We *only* had seventy-five people today" or "*Only* two hundred people showed up."

Only? I'm sorry. Are those seventy-five or two hundred people not enough for you?

I'm not going to discuss at length the perceived importance of numbers. Keeping track of "how many" is a valid metric to measure an aspect of effectiveness in terms of what we are doing. Numbers do represent people. Jesus did say that he would build his church. However, we don't always have such a clear view of what this looks like in our churches today.

Unfortunately, I think numbers have become an addiction. We flaunt our numbers, despise our numbers, fret about our numbers. Our numbers validate us. But they shouldn't. We often don't know how God is using us. We only need to know that he is — and respond with grateful hearts.

This spirit of competitiveness (whether baldly stated or merely implied) has damaged so many churches and leaders who haven't seen the same "success." After hearing it over and over, leaders who aren't as "successful" start believing the lies that maybe God just hasn't blessed them like he "blesses" other churches or leaders. And

When heaven meets the earth, we will have no use for numbers to measure who are and what we're worth.

—Sleeping at Last, "Heaven Breaks"

at that point, those leaders either shut down or begin to be driven by their need for affirmation.

When we think that our calling is to be the biggest, the most creative, or the best, we have completely lost sight of the only important fact.

We are called.

Let me clarify. There is nothing wrong with competition. There is nothing wrong with passionately wanting to show the love of Jesus to as many people as possible. And there is certainly nothing wrong with celebrating.

But if you know that you're a competitive leader, I highly encourage you to seek some honest feedback from those you are leading. You may be creating an environment of unhealthy competition, driven by your own desire to succeed instead of by God's desire to work through you.

Paul writes to the Philippians about this kind of unity through humility:

> If you have any encouragement from being united with Christ, if any comfort from his love, if any fellowship with the Spirit, if any tenderness and compassion, then make my joy complete by being like-minded, having the same love, being one in spirit and purpose. Do nothing out of selfish ambition or vain conceit, but in humility consider others better than yourselves.
>
> —Philippians 2:1 – 3

How often do we consider others better than ourselves? My experience is that it's really easy to trash-talk churches or methods that aren't what we think they should be. What is troubling is how easily I've done this and how often I've seen it done.

When I take time to reflect, I feel a vast amount of conviction about conversations I've been a part of where we've grumbled about this person, this ministry, this church. How desensitized many of us have become!

These rants (both subtle and obvious) litter our everyday conversations, blog posts, and emails. And if we are so vocally open about them, what is truly the condition of our hearts with regard to unity?

A healthy environment is formed in the spirit of true humility.

Humility that causes us to want to step out of the spotlight and take ourselves out of the picture.

Humility that makes us desire to sacrifice our own need for affirmation and acknowledgment and to bring fame and glory only to the One who made us.

Humility that not only puts God first but puts others in front of us as well.

UNCLEAR EXPECTATIONS

Adam was new to the children's team. In fact, his position was entirely new. With the rapid growth that his church's children's ministry had experienced, he hit the ground running, implementing new ideas into the children's worship services and overseeing a team of volunteers.

Because Adam jumped in so quickly, nobody really ever gave him any expectations for his position. At first, Adam thought that the lack of communication indicated a level of trust in him, and he took that responsibility and promised not to let anyone down. However, over time, Adam realized that he didn't know what his boundaries were—when it was OK to say yes or no.

The lack of clear expectations caused Adam to take a "better safe than sorry" approach to his position. He said yes to almost every opportunity that came along. Soon, Adam's wife began to notice how much time he was spending at the church on weekends. She wanted to talk to him about his being away from home so much, but she didn't want to make him feel guilty. After all, it was a relatively rare experience for Adam to discover something he really enjoyed. So she kept quiet most of the time.

Without clear communication coming from his leadership team at church, Adam began to feel overwhelmed by the tasks he faced. Was he expected to complete them all? How would he find resources to complete them? Who should he talk to in order to get the appropriate permission? And at home, he wasn't sure what his wife was expecting. He began to feel as if he was walking on eggshells.

After one particularly stressful weekend, Adam came home. His wife, who was upset because of the amount of time he had been spending at church, laid a guilt trip on him. The combination of the weekend and the tension at home caused Adam to snap. He was just a heartbeat away from calling in and quitting when he took a step back and a deep breath — and began to evaluate the situation.

Adam and his wife openly discussed what his ideal schedule would look like. And he communicated to his colleagues at church that on certain nights, he wouldn't be available.

Instead of waiting for someone else to lay out expectations for him, Adam took the initiative to put those boundaries in place so others would know what to expect from him.

Communication is essential when it comes to setting and meeting expectations. Sometimes we don't know what our leaders expect from us. Do we have the authority to take on that new project? Can we spend that money? Just when are we expected to be serving, and when can we take time to be refreshed and reequipped?

CONFLICTS IN PERSONALITY OR VALUES

Working in ministry can prove to have explosive results if we don't share key values with our team. We can work through the smaller differences, but if we aren't on the same page with regard to key issues, we put both our teams and ourselves at risk for burning out.

A micromanaging supervisor or even a gossipy coworker can put stress on your performance. Over time, this stress can build up until you shut down and stop performing. If you're on staff at a church that places a high value on financial responsibility and stewardship, but you don't think twice about spending money on the first thing that crosses your desk, you could be in trouble. Or maybe you care deeply about reaching the children in your community, but your church wants to reach only senior citizens. The cumulative effect of the stress caused by these differences can lead to burnout.

MISMATCH OF JOB SKILLS/PASSIONS

I am not what you'd call a numbers person. For me to work on bud-gets and finances — anything really to do with money — is a hard task. Fortunately, in my position, a very small amount of time is spent playing with a calculator and a spreadsheet. I still have to do expense reports, figure out budget variances, and plan how much to spend for each year, but these tasks are few and far between. We have an entire finance team who eats, sleeps, and breathes numbers. And they love it! If you put me in their shoes for a day, I'd lose my mind because I don't have the required skills, nor do I have the passion for it.

Skills can only get you so far. It takes heart to fulfill your purpose the way God intends it to be fulfilled.

OLD-SCHOOL CHURCH POLITICS

A new pastor, fresh out of seminary, took his first position as a pastor of a church. He gathered the elders to discuss the church's plans for the upcoming year. With each suggestion, he was met with the words, "Well, that's not the way we've done it before." Instead of letting this response cause tension, the pastor simply moved down his list until by the end of the meeting, he realized that not one thing he had suggested would be implemented.

Even though he didn't like to cause trouble, he did bring up the fact that they did ask him to lead and direct the church. He was answered with the following:

"My grandfather helped build this church!"

"My mother sang in this church's choir for fifteen years!"

"Our family has been tithing here since before you were born!"

Resistance to trying new things is a large stress factor for those in the church. Transitioning a church full of people who have been happy in their pews for forty years is a well-nigh insurmountable problem.

NEW-SCHOOL CHURCH POLITICS

A church doesn't have to be well established in order for it to be full of politics. Sometimes even the newest churches are filled with big visions — and equally large egos. The passion of a church planter is unmistakable. Without careful guidance and mentoring from those who have walked that road before, the church leadership team can turn into a "good ole boys" club, with the pastor leading the pack and his closest friends making all the decisions. In this scenario, there's likely no diversity and no proper confrontation or accountability. When increasing demands require the church to take on new staff or seek additional help, the new people often feel out of place and pressured to fulfill someone else's dream for them instead of the one God has given them.

NO FREEDOM TO DREAM

Early in my ministry, a pastor told me something that would forever change my outlook on dreaming. After we had met to talk about how my God-given dreams could fit into my role in the church, he looked at me and said, "Anne, your dreams are just too big for our church. Maybe it's time you found somewhere else you can dream."

Even though I was heartbroken, gradually I became inspired to prove him right. I know God's plans are way beyond what I can even imagine, so I *want* my dreams to be too big!

I realize that many of you have experienced something similar. You've been full of passion for something God has given you, only to have it shot down. You've faced the tension of figuring out how to respect those in authority over you — or to believe in your heart that those in authority should get out of the way. Maybe you are the leader, and other staff members aren't supporting you. Maybe you're being undermined. What do you do? Do you leave? Do you stay and work to be an influence?

What if you dream, and that dream dies in the hands of someone else? You begin to lose the courage to process these providential ideas, and soon, it's just easier to carry out your mundane day-to-day tasks in order to avoid getting hurt again. Even though my broken dream occurred several years ago, I still find myself extremely hesitant when it comes to expressing the things I'm most passionate about. When you've experienced this kind of hurt, it affects the way you think and dream about God, people, and especially your role in the church.

THE FURNACE

Being in ministry, you've *never* had any irrational thoughts, have you? You've never wanted to shove that annoying worship leader off the stage or shake that parent who thinks her child just *has* to be with the grade school children because he is *so much smarter* than those *other* kids in kindergarten. You've never wanted to tell your pastor off because the church has consumed all of your husband's time and now he's missed your first child's first words, first steps, and, oh my, her first date.

No, you've never had those thoughts. Because being a Christian is all about the hugs and giggles. We're smiles all the time, right?

Here's the reality: there is no perfect environment out there.

There are no perfect churches to serve in, no perfect pastors to work for, and no perfect environments.

And generally speaking, most people you run into in the church world are great, loving, caring people.

Stop laughing.

I mean that.

But I'm going to guess that more than half of you reading this at least smirked at that "great, loving, caring" line. Why?

Because you've been there — where it's not great.

Or loving.

Or caring.

At all.

And because of that, see how easy it is to be cynical?
(Says the pot to the kettle — trust me, I'm working on this one too.)

.   .   .

Being placed in a tough environment isn't something new. Around 600 BC, four gentlemen by the names of Daniel, Shadrach, Meshach, and Abednego were given positions as servants to the Babylonian government.

At first, the training they had to go through didn't seem too bad. Eat food from the king's table. Drink the king's wine. After indulging themselves for three years, they'd be ready to serve the king.

Seriously. Sign me up!

However, the men refuse the king's delicacies, probably because of the strict laws that defined what was historically "clean" and "unclean" as far as food went in that culture. This decision could have terrible consequences for the men.

Daniel tries to negotiate with one of the officials, who is worried that these Israelites' denial of the king's order will cost him his own life. But Daniel reassures him and makes the official a deal:

> "Please test your servants for ten days: Give us nothing but vegetables to eat and water to drink. Then compare our appearance with that of the young men who eat the royal food, and treat your servants in accordance with what you see." So he agreed to this and tested them for ten days.
>
> —Daniel 1:12–14

Daniel has faith in God despite unfavorable circumstances — he, along with Shadrach, Meshach, and Abednego, could have been killed for not eating what the king provided.

Yet God is in control.

And after the ten-day test, the four men prove to be stronger and smarter than those who had followed the king's orders — and they gain favor with the king.

Fast-forward a bit, and things start heating up for Shadrach, Meshach, and Abednego.

King Nebuchadnezzar decides to make an idol — a ninety-foot-tall golden idol. At the dedication of this huge statue, a proclamation is shouted out that anyone who doesn't worship the idol will be thrown into a furnace.

Well, the Ten Commandments, which Shadrach, Meshach, and Abednego followed as immutable law, clearly state, "You shall have no other gods before me." They know they have to be obedient to God in spite of their circumstance — even if it brings them to the point of death.

Being confronted by the king and later thrown into a fiery furnace as punishment doesn't sound like the most comfortable place to be, now, does it?

The king learns of the refusal of Shadrach, Meshach, and Abednego to follow his order. And he gets pretty ticked. The Bible describes Nebuchadnezzar as "furious with rage" (Daniel 3:13).

I love that intensity — the king was *furious with rage.*

And the three men — well, they tell Nebuchadnezzar that their God is strong enough to save them from the fire if they are thrown into the blazing furnace.

This is some serious faith. These three guys are about to be tossed into fire. Real, live, red-hot fire. And yet they are absolutely certain of God's sovereignty over the situation — God's sovereignty over their environment.

Their calm answer does nothing to appease the king. Instead, he gets even more fired up. He orders the furnace to be heated seven times hotter and has the strongest soldiers tie up the men.

It isn't long before the king becomes puzzled.

First, the Bible says the men *fell* into the furnace. I'm going to do my best here and assume that this isn't a tiny oven. If the king built a ninety-foot idol, who knows how big his death machine is.

Then, much to his surprise, he sees *four* men *walking* around in the furnace. The idea of *any* men walking around is crazy enough. They are tied up. The fire is HOT. The fall itself was probably enough to kill a man.

And then there's this fourth guy?

The fourth man appears to be some kind of heavenly being. The king walks over to the furnace and tells the men to come out. They do, and they are completely unharmed. They don't even smell like smoke. God has completely protected them from the blazing fire.

. . .

In ministry, we spend a lot of time in uncomfortable places. Sometimes we stand up for what we believe in, and we get shot down; sometimes we believe we're truly listening to and following God's call — and despite our best efforts, we often end up in our own fiery furnaces.

Will we trust God in the place we find ourselves? *How* do we trust God in these external circumstances?

CASE STUDY: JOHN'S FURNACE

John is someone who's been through the fire. A former executive pastor, he shared his story with me:

> I've worked in state government, a Fortune 500 company, and even a political campaign. The worst experience I've ever had at a job was working in full-time ministry. What makes this more ironic is that I raised my own salary support for the job too, so this church didn't even have to pay me.
> The mood around the office was very tense. If you messed up, you heard about it in staff meeting. Arguments were pretty frequent,

and the majority of staff thrived on conflict. However, when you're someone who doesn't enjoy conflict, it made for a very tough environment.

I was told in my interview process that family was a high priority. However, I would be reprimanded when I would occasionally take an extended lunch to attend one of my children's activities. It got to the point where my job was eventually threatened after I stayed home to care for my sick child. I hadn't been absent frequently — just twice in a six-month period.

Did I mention that I raised my own support? The threat of being fired from a job you weren't getting paid for was very difficult to deal with.

Besides the tension, it was one of the most morally uncomfortable environments I had ever worked in. The subject of sex was discussed on an almost daily basis. Staff discussed sexual positions, who in the church was "hot," who in your small group you would have sex with, if two women having sex was considered "hot," and even compared the length of a certain part of the male anatomy.

It went far beyond "guy" talk. I had never encountered that type of conversation in my career, and I have worked for some interesting people.

When I first read John's story, I was angry, sad, mortified, and extremely heartbroken. Even though I had been embroiled in some turbulent church conflicts before, nothing to my knowledge was ever publicly discussed in such a frank and unbiblical manner.

To have pastors — shepherds of a church — sharing in such an inappropriate manner was shocking to me (and being a PK, not much surprises me!), and honestly, it was just really, really creepy.

And to have your job (which you've raised your own support for) threatened for taking care of your family? Absurd — yet far too common in the church world. I know John isn't the only person out there who's heard this threat.

I emailed John back almost immediately and asked him to share more of his story. How did he survive such a terrible environment?

John wrote me back:

> This entire situation shook my belief in God and the church to the core. I would love to say that I did everything right and that I voiced concerns about inappropriate activities at every turn. Instead, I remained quiet most of the time. I didn't think that expressing concerns would do any good. I was afraid that it would just worsen my situation.
>
> My prayer life faltered, and my relationship with God wore down. I sunk into a deep depression, and I really had no connection with anyone. I was just a zombie. Finally out of desperation, I emailed a counselor friend of mine and started going to therapy. The first session was two hours long, and I was a wreck! I was diagnosed with post-traumatic stress syndrome and a moderate case of depression. We continued to meet, and I realized that the depression I was feeling was really anger I had been burying deep inside about this situation at the church.
>
> I did not feel that I had a voice, and when I did voice things, I felt they were ignored or dismissed. It has taken a great deal of work for me to get better. I quit the job, went through therapy, took an antidepressant, and really leaned on the support of my family.
>
> Work, prayer, support, and a strong foundation of faith, family, and friends were the only things that have brought me through this. There are so many times when friends I spoke to were given the right words to say to me at that time. They also encouraged me in the direction that I should go so that I could heal. I could have prayed to be healed from depression, but if I hadn't taken the necessary steps, I would have never come out of it.
>
> I don't have all the answers as to why things happened or were allowed to happen. I really came out of this with more questions than answers. However, I do realize one thing. Just because a church is growing in numbers doesn't mean it is a healthy church. A church, like anything else, can put on a great show and draw a crowd. If you're in an abusive environment, get out! Just because the environment is a church is no excuse to stay.
>
> I've also realized who I really work for. *I work for God.* One thing I discovered when I was able to break away from the situation was that I never worked for the lead pastor. I was working for God. In the end, it is God to whom I'm accountable.

A BLAZE OF GLORY

Even through the fire — through the tension, the conflict, the depression, the stress — we need to recognize that God is and always has been completely in control. Even through the most difficult circumstances,

> The circumstances of a saint's life are ordained of God. In the life of a saint there is no such thing as chance. God by his providence brings you into circumstances that you can't understand at all, but the Spirit of God understands. God brings you to places, among people, and into certain conditions to accomplish a definite purpose through the intercession of the Spirit in you...
>
> Once you have the right relationship with God through salvation and sanctification, remember that whatever your circumstances may be, you have been placed in them by God. And God uses the reaction of your life to your circumstances to fulfill his purpose, as long as you continue to "walk in the light as he is in the light" (1 John 1:7).
>
> — Oswald Chambers,
> My Utmost for His Highest

we become able to share his story, to share his healing, and to give glory to God, which is what it's all about anyway.

You may be in a great place right now. If that's the case, look around you and see who might be going through a fire. Walk alongside them. Pray for them.

On the flip side, you may be right in the middle of the furnace. Reflect back on God's faithfulness throughout Scripture. His hand is over your life. As difficult as it may be, pray for wisdom in how to rejoice within your circumstances.

The apostle Paul was probably one of the most persecuted believers in history: "I have worked much harder, been in prison more frequently, been flogged more severely, and been exposed to death again and again" (2 Corinthians 11:23).

From what Paul wrote in 2 Corinthians 11, he seemed to experience many of the same things experienced by those who serve in ministry.

> Three times I was beaten with rods, once I was stoned, three times I was shipwrecked, I spent a night and a day in the open sea *(OK, that probably hasn't happened to most of us)*, I have been constantly on the move *(check)*. I have been in danger from rivers, in danger from bandits, in danger from my own countrymen, in danger from Gentiles; in danger in the city, in danger in the country, in danger at sea *(check)*; and in danger from false brothers *(check, check)*. I have labored and toiled and have often gone without sleep *(check)*; I have known hunger and thirst and have often gone without food *(check)*; I have been cold and naked *(we'll just say cold here, OK?)*. Besides everything else, I face daily the pressure of my concern for all the churches *(Wow! Don't we all?!)*. Who is weak, and I do not feel weak? Who is led into sin, and I do not inwardly burn *(Now we're really talking!)*?
>   — 2 Corinthians 11:25 – 29, commentary added

I'm sure many of us can relate to the things Paul carried on his shoulders. What's a person to do? Most of us would cry out to God and ask for these problems to be removed or resolved. We'd ask for protection from these circumstances — or more likely for deliverance!

Even throughout his many imprisonments, even when faced with death, Paul sent letters to the churches of his day to offer hope and instruction. In a letter to the church in Corinth, he declares,

> We were under great pressure, far beyond our ability to endure, so that we despaired even of life. Indeed, in our hearts we felt the sentence of death. *But this happened that we might not rely on ourselves but on God, who raises the dead.* He has delivered us from such a deadly peril, and he will deliver us. On him we have set our hope that he will continue to deliver us.
>
> —2 Corinthians 1:8b–10, emphasis mine

You have the power, through God, to survive your circumstances; it is the same power given to Jesus through his most difficult time — his suffering on a cross. It sounds cliché, but in order to make the most of the environment and circumstances God has ordained for us, we have to rely on him.

Relying on ourselves will only cause us unnecessary pain and mess up potentially divinely appointed experiences for those with whom we come into contact. I think we all can agree that it is wise to trust God's sovereignty and continue to place our hope in him to work *in* us *through* our circumstances.

⊕ EXAM ROOM

How would you describe your ministry environment?

What are the things that make you feel out of control?

I decided not to keep my phone with me in the bathroom. What are some steps you can take to gain control over areas in your life?

In your various roles (work, service, home life), do you know what is expected of you?

Set time aside this week to clarify any expectations you're unsure of.

Even when the world seems to spin out of control, God is sovereign over what's happening. Pray that God will show you new ways of bringing glory to him, regardless of your circumstances.

Second Opinion

Mike Foster, founder of Ethur.org and coauthor of
Deadly Viper Character Assassins

A. J.: You spend a lot of time around pastors and church leaders. In general, how do you perceive the overall health of leaders today?

M. F.: I think the perception is that at first glance pastors and church leaders are doing well. They are really skilled at saying the right things and managing image. But as soon as they open up just a bit about their struggle, you realize that there is a lot of pain, depression, hopelessness, and junk. The healthiest leaders I know are the ones who are transparent in their conversations with me and honest with the issues they struggle with. And the reverse is true also. The sickest leaders I know are the ones who are hyperperfect and obsessed with pleasing onlookers.

A. J.: Why do you think it's important for leaders to take care of themselves?

M. F.: It's the only way to have long-term success. Period. If you don't take care of yourself, you won't finish well. I've known too many Christian leaders who managed churches, ministries, staffs, and volunteers extremely well, yet they could not manage themselves. And that is what sank them. I truly believe that if you are intentional and strategic about taking care of yourself, everything else will fall into place.

A. J.: In your book *Deadly Viper Character Assassins*, you talk about seven assassins that can take leaders out when their guards are down. What are they?

M. F.: The Assassin of Character Creep. This stealth assassin is all about undermining our long-term success. Often a lifetime of work can be greatly affected by a few quick, careless decisions. Leaders often engage in "character creep" as they subtly and slowly cross lines.

The Assassin of Zi Qi Qi Ren. This assassin gets its name from a Chinese term meaning "self-deception while deceiving others."

Subtly we can begin to shade the truth, refuse to face reality, and deceive ourselves. A leader begins to live with lies and travels down a slippery slope until this assassin takes him or her out.

The Assassin of Amped Emotions. Whether it's anger, jealousy, or amped-up horniness, our emotions can undermine our long-term success.

The Assassin of the Headless Sprinting Chicken. This assassin is all about maxed-out schedules and the lack of sabbath in our lives.

The Assassin of Boom Chicka Wah Wah. One word: Sex.

The Bling Bling Assassin. This assassin makes us think we are defined by our stuff and leads us to be caught up in consumerism and a materialistic focus.

The High and Mighty Assassin. Leaders often do what they do in an unhealthy pursuit of proving their worth. Ego reveals itself in a devaluing of others to inflate oneself or in believing one's own press reports. The long-term effect of this behavior is a life that comes up short and is ultimately meaningless.

A. J.: When you start feeling stressed and burned-out, what are some things you notice?

M. F.: My biggest indicator of burnout is how I treat people. Because relationships mean so much to me and are such a core of my life, if I'm stressing or burning out, this is what is impacted. If I find myself losing my patience with people quickly and my thoughts become negative toward friends and family, or I find myself withdrawing from relationships, this means I've entered a danger zone.

What's most unfortunate, and probably not a unique situation, is that I take out my stress on the people I love the most. My wife and kids have been the clear victims of my not managing my life well. That's why I've become so diligent in addressing my physical, relational, emotional, and spiritual health.

CHAPTER 5

SYMPTOMS

Are you ready? Now is the time we have to be honest with ourselves.

Remember the tantrums you would throw when you were a little kid? This is where it gets easy to focus on the negative and to make the situation worse than it actually is.

On the other hand, denial is also an enemy of the truth. We can be so wrapped up in doing — or feeling that we *have* to do — that we are afraid to face the truth that we're on a brutal downward spiral into becoming completely ineffective for the kingdom.

In this chapter, we're going to take a look at the symptoms of burnout. Most of us have probably experienced these symptoms at some point in our lives, and just because we exhibit some of these signs doesn't necessarily mean we're burned-out. And there may be symptoms unique to you that aren't on this list.

The key is honest evaluation. I think it's wise to ask for outside opinions to assist you in developing a well-rounded snapshot of yourself. If you're wondering why you're behaving in a certain way, ask your spouse, your children, or the people closest to you to provide trustworthy insight.

BURNOUT VERSUS STRESS

Sometimes we have really stressful days. And sometimes those days turn into weeks. Seasons of stress come and go.

Burnout, however, is the result of cumulative stress developed over time. Dr. Archibald Hart, founder of the Hart Institute, describes how the symptoms of stress can turn into symptoms of burnout over the passage of time.[1]

Stress	Burnout
Stress is characterized by overengagement.	Burnout is a defense characterized by disengagement.
The exhaustion of stress affects physical energy.	The exhaustion of burnout affects motivation and drive.
Stress produces disintegration.	Burnout produces demoralization.
Stress can best be understood as a loss of fuel and energy.	Burnout can best be understood as a loss of ideals and hope.
The depression of stress is produced by the body's need to protect itself and conserve energy.	The depression of burnout is caused by the grief engendered by the loss of ideals and hope.
Stress produces a sense of urgency and hyperactivity.	Burnout produces a sense of helplessness and hopelessness.

As you can see, symptoms of stress alone are fairly traumatic. As these persist without appropriate release, they worsen into burnout.

On the next few pages, I've provided checklists to help you identify some things you may be experiencing. As you work through these lists and note both the symptoms and how long you've been experiencing them, you should get a clear picture of your overall health in the four areas we've been discussing. Feel free to add other symptoms that may not be listed.

Spiritual Health

Check if you have symptom	Symptom	Duration (in months)
	No desire for Bible reading	
	No desire for prayer	
	Don't give cheerfully or sacrificially	
	Find yourself avoiding truth	
	Feel spiritually empty	
	Avoid accountable relationships	
	Lying (including little white lies)	
	Stealing (even in "small" ways)	

Physical Health

Check if you have symptom	Symptom	Duration (in months)
	Feeling tired all the time	
	Constant headaches	
	Consistent gastrointestinal issues	
	Weight gain or loss (how much?)	
	Carrying extra weight around midsection	
	Insomnia	
	Chest tightness / shortness of breath	
	Muscle aches / weakness	
	Pain in wrists or jaw (may indicate clenching hands or teeth in sleep)	

	Sighing frequently	
	Muscle twitches	

Emotional Health

Check if you have symptom	Symptom	Duration (in months)
	Easily angered / enraged	
	Snapping at small incidents	
	Negativity	
	Cynicism	
	Feeling as though you're the target ("everyone is out to get me")	
	Suspiciousness	
	Helplessness	
	Impulsiveness	
	Feeling sad	
	Lack of self-worth	
	Feeling empty	
	Don't feel satisfaction from achievements	
	Anxiety / worry	
	Panic attacks	
	Feeling as though you're on the verge of a breakdown	
	Using escapes such as alcohol, drugs, sex, or pornography	

Relational Health

Check if you have symptom	Symptom	Duration (in months)
	Withdraw from family and friends	
	Lose interest in spouse	
	Avoid children	
	Crave isolation / seclusion	
	Become anxious in social situations	
	Fear intimacy ("if they knew the real me, they wouldn't like me")	
	Find no joy in relationships	
	Dread going into work / participating in service	

OK, SO NOW WHAT?

I don't want to oversimplify things, but let's look back at your answers. Did you end up checking a lot of boxes? Have you been struggling with some of these issues for a while? Were you going through them, feeling each one intensely, saying, "Oh, my gosh, this is *so* me!!!"? Did you feel conviction setting in? Were some of the symptoms tough to evaluate?

If these last few pages are covered in pen scribble, chances are, Yes — yes, you're either burned-out, or on the brink of burnout.

Even though there is no "one size fits all" Band-Aid for healing burnout, we'll talk in the next few chapters about a few things you can do to help set you on the right path, *if you choose to work through them — and continue working through them over time.*

If you went through these lists and found that you seldom experienced the symptoms or have been experiencing some of them for just a short amount of time, you're probably not burned-out in the truest sense of the word.

HOWEVER (and yes, that's a big however) ...

You picked up this book for a reason. Something about the subject of burnout and ministry struck a chord with you. Maybe you haven't hit bottom yet, but you sense it's looming out there in the road ahead. Maybe you're beginning to experience these *stress* symptoms now, and you want to stop them now before they overtake you and Satan takes you down. The chapters ahead will help.

And finally, maybe you're not the one who's burned-out, but you care for someone who is. You could be the spouse of a pastor, the friend of a co-volunteer, or an observant staff member or volunteer who sees the culture around you taking out those alongside you. You have the ability to lead (regardless of your title or position), and you desperately want those in your care to stay healthy and productive for the kingdom.

If that's the case, the upcoming chapters can serve as a guide on how to form a healthy ministry environment and also on how to take care of yourself in the four areas of health.

Wayne Cordeiro, senior pastor, New Hope Christian Fellowship, Oahu, Hawaii

A. J.: What were the first signs you experienced that caught you off guard and made you realize you might be burning out?

W. C.: Things that once came easily came hard, such as problem solving, relationships, and preaching — they all became increasingly more difficult. I found myself getting irritable and impatient at the little things in life. I also experienced an inability to focus or make decisions on general questions.

A. J.: What did the process look like when you decided to seek help?

W. C.: I called a psychologist first and then a cardiologist. I thought I was having heart problems because my heart began skipping, and I was losing my breath. But it turned out that I was having anxiety attacks several times a day.

A. J.: Many leaders struggle with feeling that they can't take a break — fearing that if they do, something won't get done. If someone is burning out but feels that obligation, what advice would you give them?

W. C.: The first thing is to make the symptoms known to close confidants or a church board member you trust. But get help. The longer you ignore the issue and refuse to deal with it, the harder it is to detect. A diminishing of ministry capacity is next, and the longer the pattern remains, the harder it is to bounce back from the flatline. It took me three years to bounce back.

A. J.: What are some practices you've changed since your burnout?

W. C.: I don't wait till I'm fried before I take a break anymore. If you wait, it's too late. As they say in long-distance racing, "If you wait until you're thirsty before you drink water, you are already dehydrated." I also take more time to enjoy life. It is still a very difficult discipline for me since I intensely love what I do. I enjoy immensely using for God's glory the gifts that he gave me. However, an unguarded strength can become your greatest weakness. Unknowingly, the road to success and the road to a nervous breakdown became the same road.

Also, one of the best things I did was to identify those things in my life that are most important, and I invest in them each day. I run my life a bit more slowly these days, but I do it with far more traction. I have begun to strengthen my strengths as my new challenge rather than trying to prop up my weaknesses. I recognize them, but instead of driving myself to better those areas, I admit them, get others to help, and stay in my strengths. The last thing is I've learned that God has made me to be a leader, not a "manager." I was pulled in to "managing" for a few years as my main course. That diminished my leadership immune system, and I became susceptible to contagious maladies such as discouragement, exasperation, and being demotivated by others. Leaders don't catch passing emotional illnesses often, but when we are burned-out, we do. Then we isolate ourselves to keep from being affected.

PART 3

GETTING BETTER*
*DISCLAIMER: THIS MIGHT HURT

CHAPTER 6

FIVE PRINCIPLES OF RECOVERY

Some of the things I'm going to say in the rest of this book may not sit well with your comfort zone. Not to sound sadistic, but it is my sincere hope that the questions and challenges that are to come are a little painful.

Sometimes in order to heal, we have to hurt first. If you've ever dislocated your shoulder, you know this. Someone has to take hold of your arm and shove it back into its socket. It hurts like fire.

But if you let your arm stay out of its socket, it wouldn't do you a lick of good, now, would it?

If you're not ready to make some serious changes in your life right now, may I suggest you put this book down? I know I sometimes read books just to read them — I don't make any real effort to make changes in my life.

Please don't do that.

If you're content to live a completely unfulfilled life, dreading each day, feeling miserable, and, worst of all, not living the life God has given you and intended for you, go ahead and close up shop and continue wasting away. I really wish you the best, but you've got to be ready and committed to make serious changes — and make them *right now*.

If you're ready to change — if you know you can't go on living in the state you're in, with your joy completely stolen and your life being destroyed — let's continue, shall we?

Remember, there is no magic pill to help you. Chances are none of this material will be new to you. But as you commit to getting very real with a very real God and to living an abundant life, these next steps will help you begin the journey to recovery.

There are many other practical steps we'll discuss later, but I truly believe that reflecting on and taking in these five principles will provide a great foundation for making practical decisions in the future. After we become familiar with each of the steps, we'll apply them to the four individual areas of health in subsequent chapters.

PRINCIPLE I: ACCEPT RESPONSIBILITY FOR YOUR DECISIONS

I was seven years old. My parents had just purchased their first "newish" car — a 1985 Dodge Ramcharger in a beautiful midnight-blue. And with my allowance, I had just purchased a shiny metal hair clip. As I was waiting for my parents to leave church one evening, I popped the clip out of my hair and started doodling in that beautiful midnight-blue paint. I realized my clip was pretty sharp and thought I'd try to write my name underneath the door handle. Slowly I carved the letters A-N-N-E-M-A-R-I-E on the door. Before I finished dotting my "I," a friend came over and asked if I wanted to play. I ran off with her, leaving the freshly vandalized door far from my thoughts.

A little while later at home, I was minding my own business in my room. My dad came storming in, livid. He asked if I had written my name on the car.

"No," I confidently said.

He kept asking. I kept denying.

Finally, he looked down to see what I was playing with. It was a Care Bears tape recorder.

Without a second thought, he snatched it off the floor, threw it back down, and with his big size-10 shoes, stepped on it. No, *stomped* on it. Over and over and over again. Until all that was left were springs and broken pieces of plastic scattered on the floor.

I was stunned. I was angry. I was sad.

I began bawling.

He looked at me, still upset, and said, "If you would've just owned up to what you did, you wouldn't be crying right now," and left my room.

. . .

There may be many external reasons why you're burned-out. Your senior pastor could be a jerk. You may have had some difficult health issues, and now you're just trying to make ends meet because of all the medical bills that have piled up. Maybe you have genetic chemical imbalances and struggle with depression.

However, we all make choices. And the effect of the decisions you have made over time has led you now to burnout.

I'm going to say that again.

The effect of the decisions you have made over time has led you now to burnout.

That may be a tough pill to swallow. But please, let it soak in a little bit.

The first step in overcoming burnout is to own up to the decisions that have led you here.

No human is perfect. However, we do have the exact same Spirit Jesus had guiding him. The one man who endured more pain and suffering than any other man in the course of history. He definitely exhibited symptoms of stress. Sleepless nights. Desperate cries to the Father. Great temptations. Unbelievably harsh external circumstances. Yet because of his decisions, his resilience through thirty-three years of life was unbreakable.

You are responsible for the decisions you have made. The late nights. The double cheeseburgers. The neglect of your Bible, your prayer time, your family. Those were *your* decisions.

The first step on this path is *taking responsibility*. You are responsible both for the choices you've made in life and for seeking God's plan for your healing. Are you ready?

There is one exception to this rule—and a group of people whom I need to address. If you were abused—physically, sexually, or emotionally—at some point in your life, you had no choice in that decision, even though the circumstances still affect you greatly today and can even contribute to burnout.

Somebody hurt you, and regardless of the role you played in that abuse, you cannot accept responsibility for your abuser's actions. I understand the long-term effect this has on you, and I'm here to offer you some hope before we move on. Even though you have no way of changing the past or changing what happened to you, even though you were in no way responsible for what happened, you can choose how to handle the fallout that inevitably occurs.

For a brief time in high school, someone I trusted abused me. For the first few years after it happened, I medicated the hurt in a variety of unhealthy ways. The next few years, I simply blunted my emotions so I didn't have to feel anything at all. Maybe you can relate.

Recently, I met a wise and godly woman. She was my counselor, and she helped me realize that, even though I needed to let go of the guilt I was carrying in thinking that the abuse was my fault, *I needed to take responsibility for working through the pain.* It was irresponsible to cover up the hurt or ignore it. God had so much more waiting for me if only I could face the pain and the loss, grieve it, and then begin to accept the good he had planned.

In the same way, I urge you, *desperately* urge you, to take responsibility for your recovery from the abuse—no matter whether you were abused as a child or even as an adult. The truth is, abuse can occur anywhere and any time in ministry.

Accept the pain and loss and ask God to show you what he has planned for your healing. I promise he will do more in your mind and heart than you can ever ask or imagine.

Rxl

Identify specific decisions you have made that have set you up as an easy target for Satan to take down.

List some barriers to your becoming fully restored. Some examples to get you started are denial, fear of failure, and so on.

What are some steps you can take within the next week to begin accepting responsibility for your past decisions? Is there someone you need to confess or apologize to?

PRINCIPLE 2: CHANGE YOUR PURPOSE

On a stretch of highway leading to my parents' house are a series of billboards. Most of them spell out a word in giant red letters.

REPENT!!!

The word *repent* has developed an evangelical extremist stigma over the last forty years. I'm reminded of the incoherent man roaming around downtown wearing a sandwich board, screaming poorly memorized, out-of-context verses from the book of Revelation. Or I think of "repenting" from listening to "the devil's music" when I was in high school, which also led me to throw out all my country music CDs. (Notice I threw out just the country ones.)

Sometimes we do need a big billboard and giant red letters to get our attention. We need the extreme.

REPENT!!!

Repent comes from the Greek word *metanoeō*, which literally means, "to change one's mind or purpose."[1]

Let's face it: If we're not experiencing the abundant life described in John 10:10, we've gotten off course somewhere. We need to change our mind. We need to change our purpose.

Webster's Collegiate Dictionary defines *purpose* as "something to be set up as an object or end to be attained: intention, resolution, determination."

If you're burned-out, whatever it is you're trying to attain needs to be changed.

So, what is it?

Are you trying to run the best children's ministry in the country? Are you attempting to grow your church by two hundred people this year? Are you trying to make your church's print pieces the slickest in town? Have the most amazing worship service? Earn your fifth master's degree?

All of the above are extremely noble and worthy causes. You can be passionate about these things. You can run hard after them. You can do them with excellence.

But if these things are your purpose, I hate to tell you this, but …

YOU ARE CHASING AFTER THE WRONG THING!

And if you're chasing after the wrong thing — you will burn out!

Don't believe me?

Go back to pages 96 – 98 and revisit those items you checked off.

You're burned-out, right?

The only way to get back on track is to change your purpose.

What does the Bible say about our purpose?

The gospel writer Mark records for us God's greatest command:

> "The most important [commandment]," answered Jesus, "is this:
> 'Hear, O Israel, the Lord our God, the Lord is one. Love the Lord your
> God with all your heart and with all your soul and with all your mind
> and with all your strength.' The second is this: 'Love your neighbor
> as yourself.' There is no commandment greater than these."
> — Mark 12:29 – 31

It doesn't say, "The greatest commandment is to love your job with all your heart, soul, mind, and strength."

It doesn't say, "The greatest commandment is to love your calling with all your heart, soul, mind, and strength."

It doesn't even say, "Love the church with all your heart, soul, mind, and strength."

The greatest commandment.

Love the Lord your God.

With *all* your heart.

With *all* your soul.

With *all* your mind.

With *all* your strength.

And next?

Love your neighbor as yourself.

Isn't it interesting how the four areas of health we are measuring are the same areas of health God commands us to love him with, so we in turn can show our neighbors the life-changing love of Christ?

God promises us life if we obey his commands. He clearly wants to give us life. *An abundant life.*

If you are burned-out ...

If you haven't been seeking God's true purpose for your life ...

If you need to change your course and love God with all your heart, soul, mind, and strength ...

Now is the time.

Stop what you've been doing — what you've always been doing — and turn around.

Change your purpose.

There's no better time than right now.

Rx2

If you're burned-out, take a look at why. What is it that you have been chasing? Even with the best intentions, if we aren't committed to pursuing a loving relationship with our Creator, we are destined to fail. What are the things you are loving with all your heart, soul, mind, and strength?

What steps can you take this week to begin changing your course?

PRINCIPLE 3: MAKE A PLAN

In the next couple of chapters, we'll talk about practical ways to begin making changes in order to prevent burnout or to begin the journey of healing from burnout. It's very important that you make plans to change and commit to follow through with these plans.

Good intentions are great. But they won't take you anywhere. Solomon shares insight on the importance of making plans:

> A wicked man puts up a bold front,
> but an upright man gives thought to his ways.
> — Proverbs 21:29

Our good intentions are just that — a bold front. How wonderful it sounds when we say, "I'm going to wake up at 4:00 a.m. and read my Bible for two hours!" or "This is the year I train for a marathon!" Those plans may sound impressive, but they're nothing but a facade unless we put intention and action to them.

When making plans, it's easy to get overwhelmed. Patience is absolutely essential. There seems to be so much we need to work on and "fix" that it will be easy to become discouraged. It's OK to start slowly. Small steps over time can make a big difference — and not only that, God will honor your obedience in ways beyond what we can humanly accomplish.

As we make plans, we should do so with God's purpose in mind. We should seek his vision for our lives. Wise Solomon writes,

In his heart a man plans his course,
but the LORD determines his steps.

—Proverbs 16:9

Ask God to show you the decisions you need to make first. What steps are most important for you to take right now? He'll be faithful in showing you.

As the Bible teaches,

Commit to the LORD whatever you do,
and your plans will succeed.

—Proverbs 16:3

When it comes to making plans that will succeed, you must commit them to the Lord. It also doesn't hurt to write them down and commit them to yourself.

By putting pen to paper (or fingers to keyboard), you're taking your thoughts and good intentions and putting them into a tangible form. By seeing your goals spelled out, you're more likely to follow through with them. There's something about the written word that subconsciously implies commitment.

And when you commit those plans to God, if they're in line with his will, they'll succeed. It's a promise.

Rx3

This is where the rubber meets the road. You've owned up to your decisions that have taken you down the path to burnout. You've identified your course in life and have decided to get back on the right road. Now it's time to make some definitive plans. In the next four chapters, you'll be asked to make specific plans for the four areas of health. It is vitally important that you humbly seek God in prayer as you make these plans and that you commit to them by writing them down.

In the space below, ask God to begin revealing his plans for you. Jot down some initial impressions as you seek God's will. Ask him for the strength you'll need to make tough choices and to commit to whatever it is he shows you.

PRINCIPLE 4: CREATE BOUNDARIES

We want to be all things to all people. Accessible. Helpful. Always available to listen. When we're not, we think we're being selfish. What if we don't love someone the way Jesus would love someone?

Would Jesus ever say no to people?

Yes.

In Luke's gospel, we learn that Jesus spends quite a bit of time in a town called Capernaum. He heals the sick. He drives out demons. He truly exerts his authority over intense spiritual powers and shows compassion in the midst of evil. Because of this, news of his ability travels fast and far.

At the end of Luke 4, Jesus retreats. He needs to rest. He knows it's time to move on to other cities. But the people find him. They crowd him and beg him to stay.

Much more healing needs to take place. Many other people need his touch.

His response?

No.

"I must preach the good news of the kingdom of God to the other towns also, because that is why I was sent" (Luke 4:43).

Jesus wasn't sent to heal people in just one small corner of the world. He was sent to heal the world. If Jesus failed to establish boundaries but devoted himself instead to the things right in front of him, the rest of the world would suffer.

In the same way, we have to look at the entire kingdom picture when we review our to-do lists. When we see the people we "need" to talk to, the events we "must" plan, the emails that "have to be" answered …

We must ask ourselves…

Really?

Creating boundaries isn't selfish. It's necessary.

Craig Groeschel, senior pastor of LifeChurch.tv, sets a pretty amazing example when it comes to setting boundaries for his evenings. When I asked him what boundaries he had in place to protect that, he responded,

> I'm away from home one night a week — that's when I'm preaching on Saturday nights. We are literally together six nights a week as a family. The key to developing that environment is protecting our time in the evenings. I don't do evening meetings, don't schedule dinner meetings, and don't have the elders meeting in the evening. We have those meetings early in the morning or at lunchtime. I get home around 5:15 every night, and that is practically set in stone. You should design your ministry around your family values. It can be challenging because not every staff person can do that all the time, but you can to some degree.

When we create boundaries, we aren't saying to the world, "I can't help you." Instead, we're saying, "I must focus intentionally on the specific things God has placed right now in my direct influence." By saying no to people and to things that are not contained within God's distinct vision for our lives, we're actually saying yes to his sovereignty. He knows the best way for his will to be accomplished. For us to assume we can handle more is rebellious and counterproductive.

Rx4

In order to heal, you will have to create boundaries in all areas of your health. At first, expect it to be difficult when you start using one of the most important words in your healing — "NO!" You may feel guilty for saying it. People may get angry at you for saying it. But you must say it!

List three to five areas in which you know boundaries will be difficult to create and maintain. These can be about how you spend your time or how you can make changes in your relationships or in areas in ministry you know need adjustment.

1.

2.

3.

4.

5.

Write a prayer asking God to help you understand the importance of setting boundaries and to begin giving you the courage you will need to establish and follow through on them.

PRINCIPLE 5: FIND ACCOUNTABILITY

I have been forever stuck in writing this section. We recently moved, and with the move, my biweekly lunch with my accountability partner disappeared. To not be in an accountable relationship is completely unacceptable. And you can only go so long playing the "I don't know anyone" card.

So how could I write a section about accountability without having that relationship in my own life? The answer? I couldn't. For a week I have stared at this page and attempted to dream up ways to convey the importance of an accountable relationship, but God put a providential writer's block in my path.

Trust takes time. Relationships take time. And as we spent more time getting to know people in our new town, I was sure relationships would naturally develop and I'd be able to share those very personal things with someone face-to-face. But until that happened, I couldn't wait.

I emailed a friend of mine who lives in Alabama. We've known each other for a couple of years and have shared similar struggles both personally and in ministry. Also, we're both married, and we both work in a church. And most important, I trust her. I can share my darkest struggles with her. I proceeded to set up a regular time to chat about specific things we were dealing with.

When you begin the process of healing from burnout, you're going to uncover some ugly things about yourself. And you're going to want to hide these ugly things under a big rock.

That won't do you any good, now, will it?

Let's think of things that thrive in dark places:

Mold

    Mildew

        Germs

            Rats

                Smelly things

Not many good things.

The Bible is clear: Darkness and light cannot coexist.

If we keep things in the dark, we'll never be completely free of them.

Not only are accountable relationships important for areas of weakness in our lives; they're also necessary for the areas in which God is growing us.

As you work through the next chapters that deal with each area of health, you'll be asked to set goals for yourself in every area. After you set milestones, and even after you write them down, another way to show your commitment to change is by sharing these goals with another person who will ask the hard question: Are you making progress on what you said you would do?

Rx5

We need accountability in our lives. We need people to pray for us as we struggle and as we grow. As you prepare to make some long-term, life-changing decisions, identify those layers of accountability you will need to have in your life.

In the space below, make a list of those people you feel comfortable asking to help you in the process of recovering from burnout. If you aren't in any accountable relationships, write a prayer asking God to bring to your mind people you should consider. He'll be faithful in showing you — because accountability is in his plan for your life!

PART 4

A **PATH** TO **HEALTH** AND **RECOVERY**

I know I've said this before, but there are no magic pills that will help you go from burned-out and ready to throw in the towel to the most energetic and positive person in the world. We're going to discuss some practical ways to make your life healthier overall. However, I need you to keep in mind a couple of things:

- Not all of these will apply to everyone.

- This is by far an inconclusive list.

After reading many stories and realizing the breadth of how burn-out affects everyone uniquely, I had to choose the greatest common denominators. Burnout hits people in all roles and abilities, and because of the broad spectrum, I can't cover every symptom or cause out there.

What I do want to do is point you to the MadChurchDisease.com website. There you will find a forum and community that provide more focused and specific help and encouragement. It's a safe place to share your individual story of burnout and hope. I am personally involved in the forum and would love to help you work through challenges that may be unique to you or your position.

You are going to be contributing to these chapters as much, if not more, than I have. You'll have room to write and sort through plans for all of the areas of health. This should give you a solid platform for making some life-changing decisions. Remember — in the end, this change is up to you!

Everyone's journey is unique, and I am praying that as you work through issues in each of these areas, God will speak to you and reveal himself in amazing ways.

CHAPTER 7

SPIRITUAL HEALTH

> Everybody thinks of changing humanity and nobody thinks of changing himself.
>
> — Leo Tolstoy

Becoming spiritually healthy should be your primary focus in your recovery from burnout. Without this element, you can be physically fit, relationally graceful, and emotionally sturdy, but you will still be limiting the Holy Spirit's ability to work in your life.

Right now, you may be spiritually empty and dry. Your sensitivity to the sin in your own life has diminished. You know you're not in regular fellowship with God, and right now you don't even care.

Well, you might feel like you don't care, but the fact that you are reading this book is telling me otherwise.

As leaders, we are charged with the care of those God has entrusted to us. Without a high spiritual intake, our spiritual output will be low — if it exists at all. Unfortunately, because many of us are suffering spiritually, our churches and communities are suffering spiritually too.

The Bible outlines many spiritual disciplines that are essential to a believer's spiritual health. Neglecting one or more of the spiritual disciplines is probably the best way to put our spiritual health on a downward spiral. Here are five disciplines that have been vital ingredients in my own spiritual health.

PRAYER

Key Scriptures

> And pray in the Spirit on all occasions with all kinds of prayers and requests. With this in mind, be alert and always keep on praying for all the saints.
>
> —Ephesians 6:18

> Do not be anxious about anything, but in everything, by prayer and petition, with thanksgiving, present your requests to God.
>
> —Philippians 4:6

> Be joyful always; pray continually; give thanks in all circumstances, for this is God's will for you in Christ Jesus.
>
> — 1 Thessalonians 5:16 – 18

Before my trip to Africa, the longest time my husband and I had spent apart from each other was probably a week. In those times, even though we weren't physically together, we were still able to communicate on the phone or through the Internet.

However, we knew that when I was in Africa, we wouldn't be able to talk on the phone. And I honestly can't remember one time in the seven years we've known each other that we've gone more than a day without talking to each other.

After being in Africa for several days, I realized that I missed talking to Chris. Not only because I love him, but also because he understands me so intimately. I don't even have to use words for him to know what I'm thinking or feeling. He can look at the way my muscles tense up in my face and know what I'm dealing with; he can see the way my eyes sparkle when I'm dreaming something up.

Even though I was able to talk to the people who were with me on the trip, it was still difficult to process with them everything I was experiencing because, for the most part, we came into the trip as total strangers. They didn't know me as intimately as Chris does. Not being able to share even the smallest things with him on this trip caused me to shut down a little bit inside. I wasn't able to process everything completely.

God knows us even more intimately than our spouses do. And he designed us to express our deepest thoughts and longings to him. The Bible says we don't even have to use words.

When we break away from prayer, whether we consciously realize it or not, we're also breaking away from our natural design to talk and listen to our Creator. And without that line of communication flowing in both directions, we'll begin to burn out.

MEDITATION AND STUDY OF SCRIPTURE

Key Scriptures

> Do not let this Book of the Law depart from your mouth; meditate on it day and night, so that you may be careful to do everything written in it. Then you will be prosperous and successful.
> — Joshua 1:8

> I remember the days of long ago;
>> I meditate on all your works
>> and consider what your hands have done.
> — Psalm 143:5

Studying Scripture is fundamental to our spiritual health. The Bible is God's words and instructions to us. The Holy Spirit illuminates Scripture to us. We are taught about God's character. We are reminded of God's faithfulness in the past. We are instructed on how to live holy lives of love. We are convicted through Scripture.

During the times when I'm faithful, I find it hard to explain how Scripture overflows from my mind and my heart and is applied constantly throughout my day. I have personally struggled with consistent Bible study. My life seems to get too busy, and I honestly sometimes just blow it off because I'm running around "doing things for God." And during the seasons when I am lazy and neglect time in God's Word, I realize how simple it is to justify sin in my life. I lose focus on truth.

Speaking of focus, *Webster's Collegiate Dictionary* defines *meditate* as "to focus one's thoughts on: reflect on or ponder over," and the Bible shares with us the importance of both Bible study and meditation.

We typically think of meditation as something we do in solitude — which it absolutely can be. And that particular kind of meditation is incredibly essential to our spiritual health too.

Even when we're not in solitude, we are all meditating on *something*. What is it that holds your attention all day long? The psalmist realizes that we are meditators, and he directs us to the One who is the always appropriate object of our meditation:

> I will sing to the LORD all my life;
>> I will sing praise to my God as long as I live.
> May my meditation be pleasing to him,
>> as I rejoice in the LORD.
>
> — Psalm 104:33 – 34

If our thoughts and hearts are focused on things outside of God's plan for us, we'll soon lose sight of his work in our lives and in the world around us.

WORSHIP

Key Scriptures

> "Yet a time is coming and has now come when the true worshipers will worship the Father in spirit and truth, for they are the kind of worshipers the Father seeks. God is spirit, and his worshipers must worship in spirit and in truth."
>
> — John 4:23 – 24

Everyone was filled with awe, and many wonders and miraculous signs were done by the apostles. All the believers were together and had everything in common. Selling their possessions and goods, they gave to anyone as he had need. Every day they continued to meet together in the temple courts. They broke bread in their homes and ate together with glad and sincere hearts, praising God and enjoying the favor of all the people. And the Lord added to their number daily those who were being saved.

— Acts 2:43 – 47

Worship is one of those words we tend to misconstrue over time. It's become synonymous with music or a service on the weekend. So, let's just define *worship* in the context of a spiritual discipline as "expressing our dependence on the Holy Spirit by reflecting on and celebrating all of the things God has done for us and is to us." We do this both individually in our day-to-day living and corporately with other believers.

When you serve in ministry in any capacity, It's easy to become numb to the "emotion" we sometimes experience as we worship. It's easy to lose the awe Paul describes in Acts 2. And after we lose that awe, it's easy to become closed off or even cynical. Worship becomes nothing but an act, and when we go through the motions, we pull away from what God intended in John 4:23 – 24. We are no longer worshiping in spirit and in truth.

SERVICE

Key Scripture

When he had finished washing their feet, he put on his clothes and returned to his place. "Do you understand what I have done for you?" he asked them. "You call me 'Teacher' and 'Lord,' and rightly so, for that is what I am. Now that I, your Lord and Teacher, have washed your feet, you also should wash one another's feet. I have set you an example that you should do as I have done for you. I tell you the truth, no servant is greater than his master, nor is a messenger greater than the one who sent him. Now that you know these things, you will be blessed if you do them."

— John 13:12 – 17

The greatest One of all washed the feet of his disciples — including the one who betrayed him. This story is the classic example of biblical service.

Of all the disciplines, it would seem natural that service would come easily. Many times, however, we confuse self-righteous service with true service.[1]

Self-righteous service	True service
Self-righteous service comes through human effort; it delights in plans and organizational charts.	True service comes from a relationship with Jesus Christ. Energy is expended, but it is not feverish.
Self-righteous service is impressed with the "big deal"; it is concerned with noteworthy outcomes.	True service does not distinguish big projects from small, and when the difference is noted, the small task is often found to be more important.
Self-righteous service requires external rewards; it needs to be appreciated (subject to appropriate "religious modesty," of course).	True service is content in hiddenness. It does not fear attention, but it does not seek it. The divine nod of approval is enough.
Self-righteous service is concerned with results. It avoids service if the outcome might fall below expectations.	True service does not need to see results; it delights only in the service. It can serve both enemies and the ungrateful.
Self-righteous service picks and chooses whom to serve.	True service is indiscriminate.
Self-righteous service is affected by moods and whims; it exists only when there is a feeling to serve ("moved by the Spirit," as we say).	True service ministers simply and faithfully because there is a need.
Self-righteous service is temporary, mainly by way of occasional projects and "special" acts.	True service is a life-style.
Self-righteous service is insensitive. It forces itself in and demands the opportunity to help.	True service listens with tenderness and patience before acting.
Self-righteous service fractures community; once the religious trappings are removed, it focuses mainly on self-glorification.	True service builds community. It is caring and quiet and unpretentious.

Self-righteous service is service out of our own will and out of our own strength. We will burn out in no time. However, true service — the kind that is inspired by the Holy Spirit working in our lives — requires us to depend on God's strength.

SUBMISSION

Key Scriptures

"Love the Lord your God with all your heart and with all your soul and with all your mind and with all your strength."

—Mark 12:30

Submit yourselves, then, to God. Resist the devil, and he will flee from you.

—James 4:7

Submission is the enemy of our human will and the opposite of everything our hearts desire. We crave our rights. We demand our freedom.

Not our will, Lord, but yours be done. That should be our prayer.

It's interesting that in James 4:7 the biblical writer juxtaposes a sentence about submission with a sentence about the devil.

The tension between pursuing our own desires, hopes, and dreams and pursuing what God has for us can cause such confusion and distraction. And this is where Satan loves to get us every time.

The Greek word *hypotassō* ("submit") in James 4:7 has the sense of "lining up under another." Thinking of submission in a military context, we have the picture of soldiers coming under the authority of their officers. So too the apostle Paul instructs us to place ourselves in God's hands and to put on the full armor of God to be ready for spiritual warfare:

Finally, be strong in the Lord and in his mighty power. Put on the full armor of God so that you can take your stand against the devil's schemes. For our struggle is not against flesh and blood, but against

the rulers, against the authorities, against the powers of this dark world and against the spiritual forces of evil in the heavenly realms.
—Ephesians 6:10–12

It's a spiritual uphill battle to live the abundant life God has called us to. John tells us in John 10:10 that the enemy's *sole* purpose — his *only* intent — is to destroy us. However, by equipping ourselves with the armor of God and by submitting to him (relying on his protection and his power), we are promised that the devil will flee.

And we are promised life to the full.

FIGHT MAD CHURCH DISEASE: SPIRITUAL HEALTH

PRINCIPLE 1: OWN UP

1. Describe your approach to key spiritual disciplines over the last six months. Has it been constant and open? Or has it been lacking in both quality and quantity?
   - prayer
   - meditation and study of Scripture
   - worship
   - service
   - submission
2. What are some specific things you have done to contribute to the current state of your spiritual health?
3. Good or bad, do you accept your role in this?

PRINCIPLE 2: CHANGE YOUR PURPOSE

1. Sometimes we go through the motions of practicing the spiritual disciplines, but we remain empty. Identify how your purpose might be off course. Have you been lazy and

neglectful? Have you been simply checking the disciplines off a to-do list? Have you been doing them out of obligation?

2. What areas of your spiritual life need a change of purpose?

PRINCIPLE 3: MAKE A PLAN

1. Identify specific areas on which you need to refocus in order to become spiritually healthy.
2. Write down at least one way you can begin to work on the areas you listed above. Set specific goals, such as "I will read my Bible at least thirty minutes every day" or "I will participate in corporate worship."

PRINCIPLE 4: CREATE BOUNDARIES

1. Whenever we neglect spiritual disciplines, we typically do so because we've failed to create some important personal boundaries that we agree to stay within. We may be spending too much time watching television, surfing around on the computer, or simply doing nothing. Set some boundaries for yourself. For example, "I won't watch television until I've read my Bible."

PRINCIPLE 5: FIND ACCOUNTABILITY

1. Identify at least one person with whom you can share the plans you made in this section.
2. Write down a specific time and method by which you will share these plans with this person.

Matt Carter, senior pastor, the Austin Stone Community Church, Austin, Texas

A. J.: Do you see the current Western church as being ineffective in reaching people with the gospel and growing them? Why?

M. C.: Pastor Bob Roberts asked the question in a recent book, "If we (the church) could plant one thousand megachurches all over the United States over the next ten years, wouldn't we be able to completely change this country for the cause of Christ? The answer Pastor Roberts reached was, "No." Why? Because that is exactly what the church in the United States did over the last ten years. We planted over one thousand churches that have grown to more than two thousand members apiece; and yet, per capita, there are fewer people going to church today than ever before in the history of our country. Something is terribly wrong.

Why is this occurring? I think there are several reasons, but I'm personally convinced that one of the main reasons people in America are leaving the church in droves is because there is severe biblical malnourishment in the body of Christ. They're leaving in droves not because we aren't clever enough, not because we don't have enough resources, but because people come to church, are entertained, and then leave starving, anemic, and utterly ineffective for the kingdom of God. I believe this is a direct result of pastors not fulfilling primary responsibilities God designed for them through Scripture.

A. J.: What do you see as the primary responsibilities of pastors and church leaders?

M. C.: In Scripture, we see two primary responsibilities of the pastor: servants of Christ and stewards of the mysteries of God. The apostle Paul wrote, "Men ought to regard us [pastors] as servants of Christ and as those entrusted with the secret things of God. Now it is required that those who have been given a trust must prove faithful" (1 Corinthians 4:1–2). Unfortunately, so many pastors view themselves first and foremost not as servants of Christ, not as those responsible for stewarding the deep things of God to their people, but rather as *servants of the church*! I grew up in a church that expected the pastor to be available to meet the every whim and need of every congregant. If somebody was in the hospital, he better go! If someone needed to meet with him, he better be available! If he spent too much time on his sermon rather than with the people, it was said of him that he was "a good preacher" but "not a good pastor." Although hospital visitations, meetings, and coffee times with the church are important, Scripture reveals that they are not the pastor's primary responsibilities. Being a servant of Christ and a steward of the deep things of God are.

A. J.: Pastors and leaders easily assume the obligation for having to do everything for everyone, and so they neglect the necessary spiritual disciplines. What shift in thinking and pastoring is needed to mobilize the church to practice true biblical servanthood?

M. C.: The necessary shift for pastors is to come back to the primary responsibility that God intended for them. This is most clearly seen in Acts 6. After complaints had arisen within the early church that certain widows were not being taken care of (an important task, by the way!), church members went to the pastors and complained that their widows were being ignored. The response of the twelve apostles is fascinating: "It would not be right for us to neglect the ministry of the word of God in order to wait on tables. Brothers, choose seven men from among you who are known to be full of the Spirit and wisdom. We will turn this responsibility over to them and will give our attention to prayer and the ministry of the word" (Acts 6:2 – 4). So we can clearly see from Scripture that the primary responsibility of the pastor is the stewarding of the word of God so that the saints can do the work of ministry.

A. J.: How do you practice spiritual disciplines in your day-to-day life?

M. C.: I try to maximize the things that draw me nearer to Christ and minimize the things that sap my affection for him.

CHAPTER 8

PHYSICAL HEALTH

When it comes to eating right and exercising, there is no "I'll start tomorrow." Tomorrow is disease.

— V. L. Allineare

*M*oderation is a terrible word to use when discussing things like exercise and lattes and dessert and fried chicken. The word *wisdom* is much more appropriate.

We have become a society plagued by terrible physical health. I honestly don't know how we live as long as we do (maybe it's all those preservatives!). We eat when we're not hungry. We seldom exercise. We are convinced we're caffeinated robots who can thrive on four hours of sleep a night.

And we're only lying to ourselves.

Eating healthy, exercising, and getting enough sleep are the three staples of physical health. Most likely I won't reveal anything new to you in this chapter. But obviously we're pretty terrible listeners when it comes to this stuff, so maybe the refresher course, as well as the encouragement to apply the five principles we've been learning, will jump-start us into becoming a much healthier generation.

EATING HEALTHY

Key Scripture

> Don't you know that you yourselves are God's temple and that
> God's Spirit lives in you? If anyone destroys God's temple, God will
> destroy him; for God's temple is sacred, and you are that temple.
> — 1 Corinthians 3:16 – 17

It's not just Americans who eat poorly. When my husband and I were in
Scotland for a few weeks, we tuned into the BBC show "You Are What
You Eat." The host, Gillian McKeith, who is a nutrition researcher, visits
families who are overweight or obese and gets to the bottom of why.

On the particular show we watched, a very large table was covered in
sweets and junk food. Food was piled up everywhere — almost to the
point of overflowing onto the floor.

I assumed it was what the entire family ate in an entire week, but much
to my surprise, it was what *the mother*, all by herself, ate in a week.
Later, Gillian asked the parents to scoop heaping amounts of sugar into
bowls — the amount of sugar their children consumed in a typical week.
It was the equivalent of several pounds of sugar.

Many of us have developed terrible eating habits. And these bad habits
don't just affect us; they affect our children — and they'll affect their
children too if we don't call a halt.

OBESITY IN AMERICA

Take a look at these statistics from the Wellness International
Network regarding obesity in America.[1]

HOW OVERWEIGHT ARE WE?

- 58 million people are overweight; 40 million are obese;
  3 million are morbidly obese
- Eight out of ten people over twenty-five years old are
  overweight

OBESITY-RELATED DISEASES

- There has been a 76 percent increase in type II diabetes in adults thirty to forty years old since 1990
- 80 percent of type II diabetes is related to obesity
- 70 percent of cardiovascular disease is related to obesity
- 42 percent of breast and colon cancer is diagnosed among obese individuals
- 30 percent of gallbladder surgeries are related to obesity
- 26 percent of obese people have high blood pressure

So let me ask you this: *Are you a statistic?*

Time for some positive news. What happens when you eat broccoli instead of that bacon cheeseburger? Nutritionists say,

- **You fight off diseases.** By making wise eating choices, you provide your body with natural defenses against common contagious diseases such as colds and flu, and you also receive long-term benefits from cancer-fighting antioxidants and vitamins.

- **You sleep better.** Staying away from too much caffeine and other stimulants found in processed food allows your body to recognize when it's time to rest and helps you reach a deeper sleep.

- **You lose weight.** We've already talked about the harmful effects carrying extra pounds can inflict on you. Eating proper portions of healthy foods and drinking plenty of water help you lose weight.

EXERCISE

Key Scripture

Physical training is of some value, but godliness has value for all things, holding promise for both the present life and the life to come.
— 1 Timothy 4:8

I've read this verse several times before, actually thinking it dismissed the value of physical training. Let's take a look at the first part of that verse again.

Physical training is of some value …

The New Testament frequently references athletic training as a discipline parallel to spiritual discipline.

> Do you not know that in a race all the runners run, but only one gets the prize? Run in such a way as to get the prize. Everyone who competes in the games goes into strict training. They do it to get a crown that will not last; but we do it to get a crown that will last forever. Therefore I do not run like a man running aimlessly; I do not fight like a man beating the air. No, I beat my body and make it my slave so that after I have preached to others, I myself will not be disqualified for the prize.
> — 1 Corinthians 9:24 – 27

> If anyone competes as an athlete, he does not receive the victor's crown unless he competes according to the rules.
> — 2 Timothy 2:5

Exercise is a discipline. My friend Spence is one person I admire in this area. Spence, like most of us, works a full-time job. I asked him to share his average weekly workout schedule:

SUNDAY: *Run 4 to 5 miles or bike 25 to 30 miles before swim practice, which goes from 4:00 p.m. to 5:30 p.m.*

MONDAY: *30 minutes on the elliptical trainer and about 20 minutes on circuit training machines. (Optional day off.)*

TUESDAY: *Run 30 minutes.*

WEDNESDAY: *Bike 25 to 30 miles or run 4 to 5 miles; swim practice from 6:30 p.m. to 8:00 p.m.*

THURSDAY: *30 minutes on the elliptical trainer and about 20 minutes on circuit training machines, or 25 to 30 miles on the bike.*

FRIDAY: *5:00 a.m. swim practice.*

SATURDAY: *Light running (2 to 3 miles) or leisurely ride on the bike. (Mostly to enjoy the Saturday morning. If I pushed too hard during the week, I'll take Saturday off.)*

Looking at this schedule, you may think that Spence is a personal trainer or maybe just someone who's strangely obsessed with fitness. He's not. He's really just your ordinary, everyday guy who has learned the benefits of exercise. And now he loves sharing it with others.

SPENCE'S STORY

About five years ago, I started to run to lose weight. At the same time, my marriage was going through some significant challenges. Little did I know that running would help me clear my head, work through ideas, gain energy, improve my overall attitude, and give me the strength to work through marriage issues. I could think, pray, and figure things out—all in thirty minutes of running for the day. The more stressful life got, the more I ran. It was my "me" time.

My marriage ended and my life completely turned upside down. Besides the support of friends and family and my relationship with Christ, the one constant I had was running. So I turned up the heat and ran even more. I began talking to a counselor, who wanted me to consider going on antidepressants. But at a following session, he noticed a change in my demeanor. He asked if there was anything I had done differently that week to cause the positive change, and the only thing I could think of was that I had increased my running. He told me to keep on running.

A couple of months later, I read an article in *Runner's World* magazine called "Get Some Running Therapy." It discussed the positive effects running has in combating depression, anxiety, and anger. A light went off in my head—no wonder I loved running so much! It was my medication to keep me balanced and on track with healing and growing.

I felt like God had put running in my life not only to get me through difficult times, but also to teach me the discipline of training for something. My stress level is very low, and the clarity I gain is more than I could ever hope for.

Mayo Clinic lists four reasons why exercise is important in reducing stress (not to mention the overall physical benefits exercise produces).

1. **It pumps up your endorphins.** Physical activity helps to bump up the production of your brain's feel-good neurotransmitters, called endorphins. Although this function is often referred to as a runner's high, a rousing game of tennis or a nature hike can also contribute to this cause.

2. **It helps you deal with your stressors.** Exercise helps alleviate daily tensions and may also help you learn to better cope with your stressors.

3. **It is meditation in movement.** After a fast-paced game of racquetball or several laps in the pool, you'll often find that you've forgotten the day's dilemmas and irritations and concentrated only on your body's movements. As you begin to regularly shed your daily tensions through movement and physical activity, you may find that this focus on a single task and the resulting energy and optimism can help you remain calm and clear in everything you do.

4. **It improves your mood.** Regular exercise can increase self-confidence and lower the symptoms associated with mild depression and anxiety. This can ease your stress levels and give you a sense of command over your body and your life.[2]

As someone who struggles with depression from time to time, I've realized the effect that exercise has on my mood. During one of these seasons, I reached out to Gary Kinnaman, a pastor and author who has written about battling depression in ministry.[3] One of the first questions he asked me was if I had been exercising. My response was, "No." He kindly suggested I get off my "too busy" rump and hit the gym.

I knew better. And Gary was so right. Not only does exercise naturally help me get these chemicals a little more balanced, but it is also a great way to process events or frustrations. When I'm angry, I can pound it out on the treadmill, music blaring in my ears. There are few things more cathartic.

SLEEP

Key Scripture

> Unless the LORD builds the house,
>> its builders labor in vain.
> Unless the LORD watches over the city,
>> the watchmen stand guard in vain.
> In vain you rise early
>> and stay up late,
> toiling for food to eat —
>> for he grants sleep to those he loves.
>
> —Psalm 127:1 – 2

Sometimes our excitement and passion for what God is doing keep us up at night. I can certainly understand that. I've spent many sleepless nights, imagining what amazing things God could do in a situation or reflecting on something he was already doing. Other times, we lay awake at night wrestling with God, desperately crying out to him and pleading with him.

But I truly think these instances are special. I think they're exceptions to the rule. And in order to preserve their special character, I think they should continue to be exceptions.

Like the attitude we often have about not taking a vacation, many of us pride ourselves on not sleeping. We have so much to do and so much to think about that we stay up into the wee hours of the morning, convinced we can do more for God with less sleep.

I love what Psalm 127:1 – 2 says about working in our own strength instead of in God's. Cut-and-dried — if God's not doing the building, we're laboring in vain. If God isn't involved, even if we're rising early and staying up late toiling, our work is in vain.

There is absolutely nothing inherently wrong with work. There is nothing wrong with building houses (or churches or families or whatever it is you build). The Proverbs 31 woman is commended for her early rising ("she gets up while it is still dark"). Why is she commended rather than scolded for rising early to begin her day of toiling?

The Proverbs 31 woman clearly is working out of the overflow from her relationship with God. The other characteristics that define her (encouraging, wise, generous, strong, faithful, fearless, dignified) are brought to a conclusion in verse 30: "A woman who fears the LORD is to be praised."

One of the things that is easy to ignore is the fact that we are designed to rest. After working hard—physically, emotionally, spiritually, and relationally—we need rest! Otherwise, we don't just become tired; we become weary. And when we're weary, we have two choices: rely on God to refresh and renew us, or continue to operate in our own strength and burn ourselves out.

Several passages in Scripture encourage us to rest and to keep hope alive.

> "Come to me, all you who are weary and burdened, and I will give you rest. Take my yoke upon you and learn from me, for I am gentle and humble in heart, and you will find rest for your souls. For my yoke is easy and my burden is light."
>
> —Matthew 11:28–30

> "I will refresh the weary and satisfy the faint" [these are the words of the Lord]....
>
> My sleep had been pleasant to me [this is a comment made by Jeremiah].
>
> —Jeremiah 31:25, 26, notes added

> Even youths grow tired and weary,
>   and young men stumble and fall;
> but those who hope in the LORD
>   will renew their strength.
> They will soar on wings like eagles;
>   they will run and not grow weary,
>   they will walk and not be faint.
>
> —Isaiah 40:30–31

Even as we run, as we place our hope in God, we will not grow weary to the point of burning out.

And we can sleep. Without feeling guilty! Our sleep can be "pleasant"!

If you think you're immune from the medical problems caused by sleep deprivation, you are seriously mistaken. Here's a laundry list of potential problems.[4]

- aching muscles
- blurred vision
- clinical depression
- color blindness
- daytime drowsiness and naps
- decreased mental activity and concentration
- depersonalization and derealization
- weakened immune system
- dizziness
- dark circles under the eyes
- fainting
- general confusion
- hallucinations (visual and auditory)
- hand tremors
- headache
- hernia
- hyperactivity
- hypertension
- impatience
- irritability
- lucid dreaming (once sleep resumes)
- memory lapses or loss
- nausea
- nystagmus (rapid involuntary rhythmic eye movement)
- psychosis
- pallor
- slowed reaction time
- slurred and/or nonsensical speech
- weight loss or gain
- severe yawning
- symptoms similar to attention-deficit/hyperactivity disorder
- symptoms similar to alcoholic intoxication

No, you don't need sleep at all, do you?

Developing good sleep habits will help you perform better over the long haul. Breaking the bad habits you may have formed over the last several years can be tough. Here are some tips that helped me go from tossing and turning to sleeping like a baby:

- **Don't watch TV or get on the computer at night.** Some people think that TV or mindless Internet surfing helps them wind down before bed. Actually, it has the opposite effect. Did you know that the light produced from televisions and computers stimulates your mind? Your body was created to naturally associate light with alertness and dark with rest. If you stare at a glowing screen before heading to bed, you're provoking your mind to stay awake! Instead, try reading, meditating, or journaling before you doze off.

- **Keep the same routine.** Try to wake up and go to bed at the same time each night. Doing so reinforces your body's natural sleep rhythm. There's no such thing as "making up" sleep. If you stay up late, don't sleep in the next morning. Doing so will interrupt your sleep pattern.

- **Keep your bedroom dark.** The reasoning is similar to the TV and computer tip. The darker your bedroom, the deeper your rest. My husband is very sensitive to any kind of light in our bedroom. Even the smallest bit of light sneaking in under the door will cause him to toss and turn all night long. Hang heavy curtains, turn your cell phone upside down, and set your alarm clock's light settings to the lowest possible. Put night-lights in your bathroom and hallways so you don't have to turn on the overhead lights if you need to get up in the middle of the night. You'll be able to fall back asleep more quickly.

- **Relax.** This one is hard for me. My mind is always going. I've found that keeping a notepad by my bed allows me to jot down any thoughts I might have or journal any worries I'm facing. By releasing them onto the paper, I'm helping to release them out of my mind. If you're struggling with anxiety at night, find a Scripture that assures you of God's faithfulness. I've used a paraphrase of Isaiah 26:3. As I lie in bed, I repeat over and over, "He keeps in perfect peace whose mind is stayed on him." And, though it sounds a little silly, sometimes counting backward from 1,000 helps me focus and relax. I don't think I've ever gotten lower than 900 without falling asleep.

- **Cut back on the caffeine.** It's common sense, really. Do I need to explain this? Doctors say caffeine after 3:00 p.m. is a common cause of insomnia. Even if you don't feel jittery, caffeine is still a stimulant that can keep your brain from entering your sleeping rhythm.

· **Talk to your doctor.** If you've tried everything to get to sleep and you're still having issues, talk to your doctor. Some chemical imbalances can cause sleep deprivation, and only your doctor will be able to make a diagnosis. If you're comfortable taking medicine or natural supplements, perhaps you could try taking some sleep aids for a while. They can help you reestablish a healthy sleeping pattern. As you gradually decrease your dose, your body may be able to compensate and keep you there.[5]

FIGHT MAD CHURCH DISEASE: PHYSICAL HEALTH

PRINCIPLE 1: OWN UP

1. Statistically, the three main areas we struggle with in terms of our physical health are eating poorly, not exercising enough, and not getting adequate sleep. Of the three issues, do you relate to one, two, or all three?
2. What are some specific things you have done to contribute to the current state of each of these areas of your physical health?
   - eating poorly
   - not exercising enough
   - not getting adequate sleep
3. Good or bad, do you accept your role in this?

PRINCIPLE 2: CHANGE YOUR PURPOSE

1. Maybe it's convenience that causes you to skip meals, eat fast food, not exercise, and not sleep. Maybe it's pride.

Write down the underlying reason for your neglect of your physical health.

2. What areas of your physical life need a change of purpose?

PRINCIPLE 3: MAKE A PLAN

1. Identify specific areas in which you need to refocus in order to become physically healthy.

2. Write down at least five ways you can begin to work on the areas you listed above. Set specific goals such as, "I will exercise three times a week" or "I'll say no to the latte and yes to more water."

PRINCIPLE 4: CREATE BOUNDARIES

1. In ways similar to our neglect of spiritual disciplines, we often neglect our physical health because of a lack of personal boundaries that we agree to stay within. Set some boundaries for yourself in this area of physical health. For example, "I won't watch television until I've exercised" or "I'm taking the TV out of the bedroom."

PRINCIPLE 5: FIND ACCOUNTABILITY

1. Identify at least one person with whom you can share the plans you made in this section.

2. Write down a specific time and method by which you will share these plans with this person.

Shawn Wood, experiences pastor, Seacoast Church, Greenville, South Carolina

A. J.: How long have you been in ministry? And during that time, how much weight did you gain?

S. W.: The information on my driver's license (and the picture, for that matter) gives great testimony that I weighed in at a super-middleweight prize-fighting 168 pounds when I arrived at Seacoast. Sixty birthday lunches, lots of "hey, check out the leftover cupcakes in the kitchen," and many, many "I'm going to Wendy's for some comfort food" days later I looked in the mirror and realized I either had to get a new license or lose about forty pounds. Losing forty pounds is much easier than dealing with the DMV and takes less time—so I chose to go for the weight loss.

A. J.: What do you think contributed to your weight gain?

S. W.: Busyness and lack of planning would be the main two. Honestly, at Seacoast I'm not under a lot of the stresses I've been under in previous church situations. I have great people on my team—we just get too busy. When we do, we start to forget that this whole thing is a marathon and not a sprint. I started to eat fast food a ton, graze in the office kitchen, and neglect exercise.

A. J.: Were there other symptoms that resulted from your weight gain?

S. W.: Emotionally, it was a slap in the face. I still thought of myself as the super-welterweight athlete who could run four miles in under twenty-eight minutes. Then I realized that, by all official standards, I was fat. Physically, I started having some stomach problems and was put on acid reflux meds, and all in all I was just plain tired all the time. I felt like I had run those four miles every night in my sleep. And as an added bonus for my wife, I began snoring—loudly apparently.

A. J.: What was it that caused you to realize you needed to make a lifestyle change?

S. W.: What really pushed me over the edge was applying to get a new life insurance policy. Because my cholesterol was "very high," I was put in a higher bracket for "people of risk." When I realized that the insurance company thought I would die young, it scared the heck out of me. I had a new baby and a beautiful wife, and I didn't want to leave them. I chose them over Wendy's Baconator. I think it was a good trade.

A. J.: Over the course of three months, you lost forty-four pounds. How did you do it?

S. W.: My wife and I both decided to start eating right in January 2007. For the first three months of the year we ate "clean" — high-quality foods free of additives — and followed an extremely low-calorie diet. My cholesterol dropped seventy-seven points in three months, and we became an active family. In March of that year we added a gym membership, and we both still work out three to four times a week. I choose to make a date with the gym every Monday, Wednesday, and Friday at lunch — and my assistant knows I do not blow it off. I've found that the gym is much better for me than Taco Bell — who knew?

A. J.: How has developing and maintaining a healthy lifestyle contributed positively to your ministry?

S. W.: I have a ton more energy in the short run. My family life is just more active and more fulfilling as we have a ton more energy together. For the long run, I know, Lord willing, I'll be around to do ministry for years and years to come. Most of all though, and this may seem controversial, I did not do it for my ministry. I did it as an act of worship toward Jesus and as a sign of commitment to my family. If I take care of my relationship with Jesus and my relationship with my family, God will honor my ministry.

CHAPTER 9

EMOTIONAL HEALTH

It's not stress that kills us; it is our reaction to it.

—Hans Selye

You can't see emotion. I guess you can see the physical response of what someone is feeling, but none of us possess the ability to truly see into someone's heart (or brain — or wherever it is emotion comes from).

For example, if you walked into the café where I'm writing this right now and saw me typing, you probably wouldn't think much of it. I'm tucked away in the corner, occasionally sipping mineral water and casually observing people as they come and go.

What you wouldn't see is my heart racing. One of my friends had to confront someone today about some serious stuff, and I just found out it didn't go well at all. I'm hurting for my friend and the person he had to confront and the tension that now dampens their relationship.

You also wouldn't see that I'm worried. That I know there are some decisions I need to make and that I'm afraid to make the wrong one.

Emotions can fuel our decisions — good *or* bad. If we're not open to guidance and solitude, we are susceptible to letting our emotions guide us and not the Spirit.

DEPRESSION AND ANXIETY

Key Scripture

> I waited patiently for the LORD;
> > he turned to me and heard my cry.
> He lifted me out of the slimy pit,
> > out of the mud and mire;
> he set my feet on a rock
> > and gave me a firm place to stand.
> He put a new song in my mouth,
> > a hymn of praise to our God.
> Many will see and fear
> > and put their trust in the LORD.
>
> —Psalm 40:1 – 3

Stress from our decisions and even from our environment can and will impact our emotional health.

When you're in a stressful situation, your body creates hormones — mainly adrenaline and cortisol. Adrenaline typically affects your heart rate and blood pressure, while cortisol affects your digestive system.

A by-product of cortisol is delivered to your nervous system as a sedative in times of stress (that's why after certain stressful events, you feel worn-out). Over time, this can cause you to feel depressed, anxious, and helpless.

Depression that is caused by stress hormones can turn even more dangerous, physically and emotionally. You can become sleep deprived (which we've already discussed), and if left untreated, sleep deprivation can actually cause some people to develop personality or behavioral disorders. To top it off, experts say that in some cases, the actual structure of brain cells can change when these stress hormones don't go away.

Some of the most faithful people in the Bible — the psalmists, for example — struggled with feelings of extreme depression and anxiety. There is a huge stigma attached to emotional problems such as depression and anxiety (which just happen to be two of the most common emotional health challenges). Sadly, this stigma seems to especially tint the views of other believers in the church world.

We aren't filled with "the joy of the Lord," so we feel guilty. We are plagued by panic attacks, so we think we lack faith.

We also feel extremely alone. We think if we reach out for help, we'll surely be judged.

David in Psalm 40 vividly describes his feelings, but he also recalls God's faithfulness to him. He declares that his posture is such that he "waited patiently for the LORD."

If you suffer from depression or anxiety, you must get help. Pastors, counselors, and medical doctors are all people who can assist you on your journey to understanding and coping with emotional health issues. The truth is, you can't do it alone. And the healing process will take time.

It is your responsibility to seek out the help you need. And God will be faithful. His timing is never late. And it's never early either.

EMOTIONAL ESCAPISM

Key Scripture

> I hold fast to your statutes, O LORD;
>   do not let me be put to shame.
> I run in the path of your commands,
>   for you have set my heart free.
> Teach me, O LORD, to follow your decrees;
>   then I will keep them to the end.
>
> —Psalm 119:31 – 33

God has created us to be emotional beings. When we're hurting, we often think that changing our physical circumstances will fix our emotional response. That's when we get into creating unhealthy emotional escapes.

In the years following the time I was abused (which was shortly after my family had left the church), I felt empty. At the time, I didn't fully understand all that had happened. All I knew was that the pain and isolation I felt was indescribable. So I did what anyone would do — I escaped.

In the beginning, my escape was in the form of unhealthy relationships with men. I would do anything in order to be affirmed. I needed to feel worthy and loved. After a few years on that road, I realized I only felt emptier and more isolated. I started drinking alcohol. And when that wasn't enough, I would combine the alcohol with prescription anxiety medicine.

It numbed my pain alright, but it didn't allow me to work through It.

Over time, I stopped abusing the alcohol and medicine. I met Chris, and we got married. My escape then turned into something a little less obviously sinful — but sinful nonetheless.

I became a workaholic.

Being productive became my escape. It covered up the emotions I still hadn't dealt with. It was only about a year ago, in a counseling session, that my therapist started pulling the bits and pieces of my past out of my heart. And with it came a lot of pain. Pain I had been hiding and allowing to build up over the last decade. Pain I didn't even realize existed. I had been living with it for so long that it had just become part of who I was — and so I simply accepted it.

It was strange. My first instinct was to go find the biggest bottle of wine (OK, whiskey) and drink it until I didn't feel anything anymore. I hadn't felt that urge in a long time. I told my counselor this. And she helped me realize I was only trying to escape again. It was a completely natural reaction.

She wouldn't let me. Chris wouldn't let me. Others around me who knew of the situation wouldn't let me. Over the course of a few months, I was able to face that pain. Feel it deeply, all over again. But I was able to work through it.

The key in escaping is *where* you run.

Do you run to something that only covers up your pain? Something that allows you to hide in it?

Or do you run to God?

Do you escape to his healing power?

To his mercy?

To his grace?

If you're escaping from something right now in an unhealthy or immoral way, you may be a bit scared to talk about it with someone. What will happen to your ministry if you confess? You could be escaping into pornography (on TV, on the Internet, or through just dwelling on images in your head—you don't need a screen). You could be having an inappropriate relationship with someone—emotionally or physically, or both. You could be using alcohol or nicotine or weed or Xanax as the place to which you run. Internet chat rooms? Gambling? Eating disorders?

Whatever it may be, you've got to stop escaping *now*. You may lose your ministry or your reputation. So what? Right now, it's a lie anyway. There is healing and grace in confession. There is power in truth.

The truth will set you free. And that's the only thing that will.

FIGHT MAD CHURCH DISEASE: EMOTIONAL HEALTH

PRINCIPLE 1: OWN UP

1. Sometimes the decisions you make affect your emotional health, and quite honestly, sometimes it has nothing to do with your decisions. However, you are responsible for getting help. Are you ready to be honest about your emotional condition?
2. Are you struggling with depression, anxiety, escapism, or something else that's contributing to your emotional burnout?
3. What are some specific things you have done to contribute to the current state of your emotional health?
4. Good or bad, do you accept your role in this?

PRINCIPLE 2: CHANGE YOUR PURPOSE

1. If you are suffering from an emotional disorder, describe what things are like for you right now.
2. How does where you'd like to be contrast with where you are right now?
3. What areas of your emotional life need a change of purpose?

PRINCIPLE 3: MAKE A PLAN

1. If you're not already seeking help for your emotional well-being, now is the time to begin. Identify the people who can help you begin to get healthy again. Circle any below whom you can seek out this week.

Pastor   **Friend**   **Counselor**

          Doctor   **Other** _____

2. Set specific goals for your emotional health. For example, you may seek to talk to a counselor or pastor a set number of times per month, journal about your emotions, see a doctor and try a medication, or meditate on how to run toward Christ.

PRINCIPLE 4: CREATE BOUNDARIES

1. Setting boundaries can help us focus on where we need to grow in our emotional health. Are there any relationships that are causing undue stress and therefore really need to be addressed by you? Do you need to have boundaries to help you avoid unhealthy escapes? List below the boundaries and how they will keep you from choosing the way of escape.

PRINCIPLE 5: FIND ACCOUNTABILITY

1. Identify at least one person with whom you can share the plans you made in this section.
2. Write down a specific time and method by which you will share these plans with this person.

Gary Kinnaman, pastor and author,
Phoenix, Arizona

A. J.: You've thoroughly researched and openly discussed your experience with depression. What are some causes of depression?

G. K.: In our book *Understanding Depression and Finding Hope*, my coauthor Rich Jacobs, MD, and I demythologize depression, and we uncover two terrible myths. First, people commonly believe that antidepressants are mood-altering drugs. You know, pop a pill, and you'll feel fine in no time. Antidepressants don't work that way. Instead, they slowly "heal" a person's brain chemistry. If they were mood altering, you could buy them on the street! I can feel a half a glass of wine in my head in minutes. But an antidepressant? There's no buzz. I've taken 'em, and weeks later I'm still wondering if they're helping — until one day my wife says, "You've been so much easier to live with lately."

The second myth: Depression is caused by bad things happening in your life, like losing your job. Yes, everyone "feels" depressed when bad things happen. And when things get better, they feel better. Or maybe they were able to overcome their feelings of depression by getting their minds off their loss. Some have called this acute depression. In our book, we call it simple discouragement.

"Feeling down" is a common human experience, so we have difficulty understanding others who suffer from chronic or clinical depression, which is not essentially related to external circumstances. People who are chronically depressed can't just pull themselves out of it. Certainly, negative events can exacerbate clinical depression, but clinical depression is inside out — often the result of a chemical imbalance, the exact nature of which can be elusive.

A. J.: What first signaled to you that something wasn't right?

G. K.: I have a family history of depression, so the way I felt, as early as high school, just seemed "normal." For years, I lived with a residual darkness, especially when I got up in the morning, a mild form of chronic depression called dysthemia. I prayed. I fasted. I got prayed for. I got a health food store full of advice. I exercised. But in the morning, oh, I was heavy inside.

A. J.: Did suffering with depression change the way you did ministry?

G. K.: I don't think so. But it certainly changes one's perspective on God and ministry. All of us have some dysfunction — a euphemism for sin and fallenness — and anyone in ministry has to face their own "demons," be realistic about them, and let God's grace minister to them and through them.

It's like Peter after his denial: "After you've gone through this," Jesus said (and I paraphrase), "strengthen your brothers." How do you strengthen anyone after you've just had the worst night of your life? You realize you have nothing to offer but Christ in you. "We have a treasure in clay pots," Paul wrote. I realized long ago that I could not minister out of some kind of perpetual spiritual euphoria. I've had to learn how to serve God obediently and faithfully.

It has been said of Abraham Lincoln that, today, he would be declared unfit for public office. Yet, ironically, many believe it was his melancholy that empowered him, yes, empowered him, to lead the United States during the dark years of the Civil War. Lincoln, like no other in his time, was deeply empathetic with those who suffered on the battlefield, yet resolutely realistic about what had to be done to win the war. Shouldn't Christian leaders demonstrate these same qualities?

A. J.: People who are hurting often use escapes such as drugs, sex, or workaholic tendencies to cope with their pain. What are some healthy alternatives?

G. K.: In our book, Rich and I identify a number of practical approaches to treating depression. Among them are medication, therapy, Bible reading, prayer, self-talk, changing your thinking patterns, safe relationships, exercise, diet, even spiritual warfare at times. Depression is a comprehensive problem that requires holistic treatment.

A. J.: Many times, people feel alone or guilty because they have depression, anxiety, or other emotional illnesses. What would your advice to them be?

G. K.: I read recently — and I should have known this, given my two seminary degrees — that one of the original seven deadly sins was melancholy. Yeah, depression was considered a sin of the worst kind. Thankfully, the Catholic Church changed this a couple of hundred years ago when they replaced melancholy with sloth. Yet it's still not uncommon today to hear people say something like this: "Anyone who is persistently depressed is missing something in their relationship with God." Indeed, people have questioned Mother Teresa's salvation because, as she confessed, she felt distant from God and empty inside for most of her life.

To emote is human; to love those who emote is divine. Like some people who are better at baseball, or writing, or chemistry, some of us are just better — or worse — when it comes to emoting. Adam and Eve were naked and not ashamed. I've come to "accept" my depression as a part of the fallenness of my soul. And I am not ashamed. In many ways it's made me a deeper Christian and a better human being. I've heard the same voice that spoke to Paul: "My grace is sufficient for you." And it's made me less depressed!

CHAPTER 10

RELATIONAL HEALTH

There's one sad truth in life I've found
While journeying east and west—
The only folks we really wound
Are those we love the best.
We flatter those we scarcely know,
We please the fleeting guest,
And deal full many a thoughtless blow
To those who love us best.

— Ella Wheeler Wilcox

When we burn out, our created instinct toward community also fizzles. In Genesis 1:26, God declared, "Let us make man in *our* image." We are designed for relationships.

UNNECESSARY TENSIONS IN RELATIONSHIPS

Key Scripture

Better to live on a corner of the roof
    than share a house with a quarrelsome wife.

—Proverbs 21:9

For some reason, this verse always makes me laugh. And whenever I get an attitude with Chris, I think of him camping out on our roof. It cracks me up every time. Maybe God's intent for painting such a vivid picture was to help us loosen up when we begin to take ourselves too seriously.

Stress and burnout can cause us to project our pain and exhaustion on others — usually on those closest to us. Some people respond to burnout by lashing out in anger — storming around in a rage as their lives are falling apart.

Exhaustion can cause us to shut down and stop communicating with our spouse or our friends. And by *communicate*, I mean both talking and listening. We no longer feel connected to those around us, and we begin to not care about nurturing those relationships God has placed in our lives.

After not communicating for a while, resentment can develop. Our spouses or friends may not feel comfortable opening up to us anymore, and bitterness can be formed and directed toward us, toward the church, and even toward God.

In Matthew 5:9, Jesus directs us to be "peacemakers" (in Greek, *eirēnopoioi*, from *eirēnē*, which means "peace," and *poieō*, which means "to do or to make"). It will take effort and intentionality on our part to bring balance back into our relationships. We are to make peace and strive for unity.

INAPPROPRIATE RELATIONSHIPS

Key Scripture

"You have heard that it was said, 'Do not commit adultery.' But I tell you that anyone who looks at a woman lustfully has already committed adultery with her in his heart. If your right eye causes you to sin, gouge it out and throw it away. It is better for you to lose one part of your body than for your whole body to be thrown into hell. And if your right hand causes you to sin, cut it off and throw it away. It is better for you to lose one part of your body than for your whole body to go into hell."

— Matthew 5:27 – 30

Burnout, in its most extreme cases, can push us to escape into inappropriate relationships.

Deep inside us, beyond anything we can comprehend, understand, or express, there is a need. This need presents itself differently, because we are unique individuals. For someone, it may be security; for others, it may be acceptance. Or affirmation.

Regardless of how these needs manifest in our lives, they all exist for the same reason. We need to feel loved. We need to be accepted. We need to feel worthy.

It's an ache nobody can fully verbalize. But you know what it feels like. It's an emptiness. A burning. A resonating hollowness that resides so deep within your chest that you wonder how such a small space could accommodate such an infinite longing. It's like having all the air knocked out of you, but you continue to breathe in and out.

Looking at it logically, it should be easy enough to appease the desire this need places within us. I mean, if you believe the Bible, it pretty much sums it up in one verse in Philippians:

"My God will meet all your needs according to his glorious riches in Christ Jesus" (Philippians 4:19).

And if you throw in a spouse:

"The Lord God said, 'It is not good for the man to be alone. I will make a helper suitable for him'" (Genesis 2:18).

When you go through premarital counseling, one of the things counselors seem to be required to teach you is that your spouse is supposed to be your companion, and she is supposed to meet your needs. However, they always throw in the little disclaimer — "For those needs that aren't met, you should rely on God to meet them."

So sum it all up — and according to what we're taught, there shouldn't be a needy one among us. For those earthly desires, we have our companion and soul mate. And in case this falls through, God's a great safety net.

Right?

If only life were that simple. We are frail and fallible human beings.

It's not easy for Chris to meet my need for affirmation. Does he affirm me? Absolutely. More than I often give him credit for. But growing up without much affirmation, I know that the longer this need goes unmet, the harder it is to satisfy.

And when I'm burned-out, my defenses are down. If it weren't for other methods of accountability I have in my life, I could fall (and have occasionally fallen) into a serious trap.

The power of this deep human need is probably one of the most compelling forces on this earth. I know I've let it run my life on more than one occasion. It has the potential to remove all sense of responsibility, of commitment, of reality. It releases your mind into a fantasyland where you feel completely fulfilled because you're valued.

Satan knows we're vulnerable in this area. And he'll throw anything in our path to tempt us. He will nudge us to feel worthless. He'll fuel a cycle of negative thoughts in our mind. And then he'll present us with opportunities to receive that validation elsewhere, which we can and should only find in Christ.

Emotional affairs.

> Physical affairs.

>> Codependency.

We must do everything we can to protect our relational integrity.

ISOLATION

Key Scripture

> The LORD God said, "It is not good for the man to be alone. I will make a helper suitable for him."
> —Genesis 2:18

When we burn out, we feel like we don't have anything to offer relationally.

And sometimes, we don't even want to let people peek into our lives out of fear that they'll see the mess and run.

In 2004, the National Opinion Research Center conducted a survey in which it found that Americans are increasingly lonely and isolated. According to the survey, nearly 75 percent of people in 1985 reported they had a friend in whom they could confide, but only 50 percent in 2004 said they could count on such support. Lynn Smith-Lovin, a Duke University sociologist who helped evaluate the results of the survey, said, that increased professional responsibilities, including working two or more jobs to make ends meet, and long commutes leave many people too exhausted to seek social — as well as family — connections. "Maybe sitting around watching 'Desperate Housewives' ... is what counts for family interaction," quipped Smith-Lovin.[1]

I'm naturally an introvert and a bit shy as well. For me to go and seek out new relationships is challenging. In fact, it's an area in my life where I have to trust God right now, and it's difficult to be obedient.

Even though he'd disagree with me, my husband is much more natural when it comes to relationships. I think it's because he's a little (OK, a lot!) more laid-back than I am. He is not a perfectionist. I, uh, can be. He's not worried when others see the areas where he struggles. My first inclination is to clam up and hide.

Isolation isn't just unhealthy for us relationally. It also has a huge physiological impact. One study found that the magnitude of risk associated with social isolation is comparable with that of cigarette smoking and other major biomedical and psychosocial risk factors.[2]

We are made for each other. It may be difficult to step out of your isolation, but I pray that you will see God's faithfulness as he provides you with the relationships you need.

I'm trusting him right now for this.

Will you trust with me?

FIGHT MAD CHURCH DISEASE: RELATIONAL HEALTH

PRINCIPLE 1: OWN UP

1. Are you isolating yourself from relationships? Are you having problems communicating in your marriage? Are you involved in an inappropriate relationship? List the areas where you are relationally unhealthy.
2. What are some specific things you have done to contribute to the current state of your relational health?
3. Good or bad, do you accept your role in this?

PRINCIPLE 2: CHANGE YOUR PURPOSE

1. God has created us to be in community with others. If you are struggling in your relational health right now, why is that?
2. What areas of your relational life need a change of purpose?

PRINCIPLE 3: MAKE A PLAN

1. Do you have relationships you need to work on by becoming more available and participating socially, taking steps to improve communication in existing relationships, or ending relationships that aren't healthy?
2. Set specific goals for your relational health.

PRINCIPLE 4: CREATE BOUNDARIES

1. Not having enough time is one of the biggest reasons people become isolated or can't invest in relationships. What are some areas in your schedule that need adjusting in order to make time for more quality relationships?

PRINCIPLE 5: FIND ACCOUNTABILITY

1. Identify at least one person with whom you can share the plans you made in this section.
2. Write down a specific time and method by which you will share these plans with this person.

Brandi Wilson, pastor's wife, Cross Point Community Church, Nashville, Tennessee

A. J.: What do you see as your greatest calling in being the wife of a pastor?

B. W.: I think my greatest calling is to encourage and support the staff. They are performing a daunting job that can consume a lot of their time, energy, and attention, and I feel called to "love on them" (such a Southern phrase). It might be as simple as an email letting them know that worship was great the previous Sunday. Or remembering to ask about a situation occurring in their family. I also want the staff member's family to know that we value them. We like to work on strengthening those relationships outside the walls of the church. We'll plan social events together, such as enjoying dinner together, hanging out at the pool, or grabbing ice cream after church. At Cross Point we put a huge emphasis on community, and I feel that my role is to help create and nurture that sense of community among the staff.

A. J.: As the church grew, how did your role change?

B. W.: My role as pastor's wife hasn't changed much as the church has grown. Thankfully, we've never served in a church that expects a typical pastor's wife, which works great for me because I'm allowed to define my role. That alone gives me the ability to serve in a ministry that aligns with my gifts and my passions rather than filling a spot because it is expected of me.

As Cross Point has grown, I've realized how much the congregation just wants to feel like they know our family. They'll attend a church of two thousand and know very few people, but they want to feel like they know us. They like to see that we're real people with real problems, facing the daily challenges that everyone else faces. People come to church looking for authenticity, and they love seeing that authenticity lived out in the pastor's family.

A. J.: What kinds of boundaries do you set to protect time alone with your husband?

B. W.: With three small children we have a hard time being alone, but we guard our family time very carefully. What works for us is specifically setting time aside on the weekend for our family. That family time might be spent at home, at the ballpark, in the front yard, or even with friends, but it's definitely away from church activities (as much as we can control). Our weeks from Sunday to Thursday are usually jammed full of "life," and we both love knowing that we have some quality time coming on the weekend. Since we both thrive on being able to disconnect, we focus on weekends to reenergize us.

Another boundary that helps protect us is working hard not to "talk church" at home. We might discuss the surface stuff, but I know that when Pete gets home, he has talked, thought, and worked church all day and just wants to be home — the place he knows is his refuge. So we usually discuss the "how was your day details" and then move on to life outside of Cross Point. I trust that if anything major is going on, he'll fill me in (it has taken a lot of practice for me not to drill him with questions, and I still fight it sometimes). Pete is encouraged by knowing he's not going to have to rehash his workday with me unless *he* chooses to revisit the day.

A. J.: What has been the most challenging part of public life and ministry for your family?

B. W.: The most challenging part is the expectations. Expectations go along with any job, but no one thinks *pastor* and then thinks "good time." People don't expect you to actually be someone they would enjoy hanging out with. They expect you to be stiff and full of rules. When people learn of Pete's occupation, we get varied responses. For instance, we've had neighbors who have built a privacy fence between our house and theirs, neighbors who have told us to never invite them to church, even neighbors who, after finding out that Pete worked for a church, have never waved hello again. But along with that, we've had neighbors Pete has baptized, neighbors we've been in community groups with, and even neighbors who say that Cross Point has helped to keep their family together. The good far outweighs the bad.

I do worry about how those expectations will affect my children. Being raised as PKs adds another level to the normal expectations of life. We're not going to allow other people to pressure our kids into fitting a certain mold.

A. J.: Why are relationships and community essential for you as a pastor's wife but also for believers in general?

B. W.: When someone asks me for my view of the best part of ministry, I always answer, "People" (they can be the worst part too). When I look back on our years in ministry, I always think about those special people who came alongside us as friends. We couldn't have made it this far by ourselves. We've needed those relationships to encourage us, support us, and remind us to keep our chins up. The thing I love about the way we do ministry is the fact that we don't do it to "bring home the bacon." What makes us do ministry — and love doing ministry — is the community. Cross Point isn't just our church, a place where we worship on Sunday. When we talk about Cross Point, it isn't a building; it's the community we do life with. It's the people we vacation with, the people we pray with, the people who call and ask about how our day went, the people who love our children, the people we can go to in times of trouble and in times of joy. They aren't just faces we see on Sundays, but people we come alongside and walk through life with.

Those relationships aren't just needed in ministry; they're needed in everyday life. I believe we are called to be committed to one another as believers in order to experience dynamic faith. Finding authentic relationships and a community that engages in biblical truth is life changing.

CHAPTER II

PROCESSING THROUGH PAIN

Why does it seem as though when another believer hurts us, the pain we experience is exponentially greater than if we are hurt by someone who doesn't share the same faith?

I wish I had the answer to that question, but I don't. All I know is that it's true, and the pain can be paralyzing. I wrote in the introduction that we weren't going to focus on the pain, but it *is* something that needs to be addressed. Now is the time.

In earlier chapters, I told a bit of my father's story and how being a preacher's kid affected me. Was I hurt? Did the actions of others cause pain to our family? More times than I could possibly write about.

But do I wish I had been protected from experiencing that pain?

Honestly, no.

One of the most frequently asked questions I get is from pastors concerned about protecting their families from seeing the brutality that often occurs in churches: "How can I protect my kids?"

And then they ask me, "What do you wish your parents had done differently?"

Not a darn thing. Seriously. I almost wish they had let me see more. I think it would have given me a healthier perspective — and a more realistic expectation — of what the dark side of the church can be like.

The most painful experience of my life happened during a time when I was in leadership at a church. My heart was severely wounded by a fellow staff member. Even years later as I write this, I have to be careful not to let bitterness creep back in.

What happened? Long story short, I opened up to a staff member. I shared my dreams, and he discounted them. I shared my weaknesses, and he exposed and exaggerated almost every one of them inappropriately to several other staff members. He lied and manipulated people on my team, sometimes plotting to turn us against each other. He set me, and others, up to fail.

After being wounded, I wanted to throw in my ministry towel. Every reason I had for avoiding the church had been confirmed. My husband and I tried to remain involved in that church, but it was too painful.

Some of our dearest friends were involved in ministry there. They had questions about what happened, and in order to preserve some sort of unity, we wouldn't answer them specifically. We left. And that was painful too.

The process of healing from this experience is ongoing. It's taken several years so far, and I'm guessing it's something I'll always have to deal with from time to time.

And if you've been hurt, you know the range of emotions you walk through.

Anger

                        Sadness

               Loneliness

      Doubt

                                 Fear

It's almost impossible to trust again.

So, what happens now? Maybe you were hurt yesterday, or perhaps it was twenty years ago. I don't pretend to have all the answers. But I will share with you some parts of my own journey that God has certainly redeemed.

PRESERVING UNITY

One of the mistakes a lot of people make when they've been hurt is to lash out. I made this mistake frequently. Once, I was literally trembling with anger after a meeting with the aforementioned staff member. As soon as it was over, I went into my friend's office and exploded, completely tearing my adversary apart. I trashed his leadership, his motives, and his authority. My friend, older and wiser than I am, calmly let me empty all my barrels.

After I tearfully finished, he shared an experience he had gone through at another church. He had been unjustly let go. But he and his wife decided to take the high road. They had plenty of opportunities to trash-talk their former church, but they refused to do so.

Before talking to my friend, I thought my only option was to lash out and expose this staff member for who he really was. The world needed to know. Or so I thought. But now, I was presented with the clear alternative — to keep quiet about the things that upset me, and move on.

It isn't easy to keep your mouth shut when someone unfairly betrays you. But except in rare occasions — when someone's health or immediate well-being is at stake, for example — it's necessary for the sake of unity.

Some of the greatest leaders I know have been severely hurt in ministry. I interviewed several for this book, and I discovered this consistent insight: the leaders who were the healthiest were the ones who never disrespected the people who hurt them.

Did they admit their hurt? Did they tell me their stories? Absolutely. But they also preserved unity. Being hurt is extremely painful. But we can't let our emotions dictate our actions.

TALKING ABOUT IT

Even though it's unwise to react emotionally and dishonor someone who has hurt you, it's extremely unhealthy not to discuss it. The key to doing this in an honoring manner is to find a mature and wise person who will look at the situation objectively.

What "talking about it" doesn't mean is fueling gossip with your friends. You may need to find someone outside of your church to talk to. My own process led me to get counseling at a faith-based counseling center on the other side of town.

Because my counselor was board certified, she was required by law to keep what I said confidential. It was an extremely safe place to unload, at times emotionally, about the pain. And since she was outside of the church's circle, her objectiveness encouraged me to look differently at facets of my situation.

One of the most striking things I learned by talking to an objective person was that the person who was hurting me was clearly also hurting as well. Recognizing this commonality somehow allowed me to see his humanity and brokenness instead of only the pain he caused me.

PRAYING ABOUT IT

Working with a counselor also helped me pray for the person who was hurting me, which wasn't an easy task. But doing so was necessary for my growth.

Praying for this person was literally a life-changing experience. It not only helped me by taking the focus off myself but also brought me closer to the heart of God — which is exactly where I needed to be in order to truly love someone I considered an enemy.

FINDING STRENGTH TO FORGIVE

For me, the hardest part of this process has been forgiveness. It's not a onetime decision. In a way, it's like marriage. It's a commitment you make for the rest of your life, because, chances are, you're going to remember significant pain indefinitely.

I wasn't sure how to forgive this man, but I knew it was something I had to do because I wanted to follow Jesus' example of ultimate forgiveness. I no longer wanted to be a slave to the negative emotions in my spirit.

And choosing to forgive him meant abandoning the myths and learning the truth about forgiveness.

Forgiveness Myth #1: You Can Forgive and Forget

Many people think the phrase "forgive and forget" is an ancient proverb, rich with wisdom. Actually, it comes from Shakespeare's *King Lear*: "Pray you now, forget and forgive." Some offenses we're able to forget, but most of the time, there are things that can never be erased from our memories. Unfortunately, anything short of a lobotomy can't guarantee us the mental deletion of something that has hurt us. What's important is how we respond when these memories surface. Do we resort to bitterness and anger, or do we lean into our heavenly Father's arms and draw from his love to heal the wounds?

Forgiveness Myth #2: You Can't Forgive without Hearing "I'm Sorry"

One of the biggest issues I struggled with was the fact that I never received an apology. Whenever I would see my coworker at church after I had resigned from my position, he acted as though nothing was wrong, which only intensified my resentment toward him.

An apology never came, and assuming that he wasn't sorry for his actions made it difficult for me to even *want* to forgive him. Throughout the course of my healing, whenever I feel cheated, I reflect on a story that Jesus taught when asked about forgiveness.

A servant has become seriously indebted to his king — somewhere around the sum of $10,000,000. Moments before he, along with his family, are to be sold into slavery, he begs the king for another chance. Touched by his plea, the king releases him from his indebtedness.

After the pardoned servant leaves, he runs into a fellow servant — one who owes him only about $10. He immediately confronts him, demanding the money he's owed. The other servant isn't able to pay him back, so instead of pardoning the debt, the first servant throws his debtor into jail until he pays up.

The king finds out about the situation and is outraged: "Then the master called the servant in. 'You wicked servant,' he said. 'I canceled all that debt because you begged me to. Shouldn't you have had mercy on your fellow servant just as I had on you?'" (Matthew 18:32–33).

Yes, it is difficult to forgive someone who has hurt us, but I think of how many times I have been pardoned when I didn't deserve it. I think of how gracious others have been toward me, and how much Jesus sacrificed for my redemption.

By waiting for an apology that may never come, I was allowing this man's lack of action to control my decisions. To truly grow through this experience, I had to decide to forgive him, whether or not he ever asks for it. I have to extend to him the very grace that is extended to me.

Forgiveness Myth #3: Forgiveness Is a Feeling

After being hurt, it's natural to want to feel somewhat normal again. Instinctively, we want to do whatever we can to get rid of the pain and forget what happened. It's easy to deny the pain and try to hide it in the back of our minds. We occupy ourselves with activities or other relationships in order to avoid feeling the heartache. Or maybe we numb the pain by abusing alcohol or drugs.

I initially allowed my feelings to hold me back from forgiving my coworker who hurt me. I decided I wasn't ready to forgive him. In the midst of the pain I continued to feel, I convinced myself that when the time was right, I would know it, because I would be emotionally able to let it go.

However, after being hurt, we may never *feel* ready to forgive someone. When forgiveness is necessary, it means that someone has caused us pain. Forgiveness is deciding to move on in spite of our emotions. The more quickly we can begin the process of forgiveness, the less control we allow our pain to have in our lives.

Jesus set a consistent example of forgiving quickly. He said to the paralyzed man, "Take heart, son; your sins are forgiven" (Matthew 9:2), without the man even asking for forgiveness. As he was hanging on a cross, Jesus forgave those who crucified him without them seeking it: "Father, forgive them, for they do not know what they are doing" (Luke 23:34).

Our heavenly Father knows us intricately — inside and out. He knitted together the very fibers of our being, including our spirit. He wants nothing more than to be close to us. He knows that when we refuse to forgive, the bitterness that results will saturate our soul. As time passes, we begin to lose the ability to recognize his gentle touches in our lives. Before long, we isolate ourselves from the only One who will never bring us harm.

Throughout Scripture, we find example after example of forgiveness. God knew it wouldn't be easy for us to forgive, and he offers us the courage we need to extend forgiveness and the strength we need to heal. It's up to us to take the first step and begin the journey of forgiveness.

TRUSTING AGAIN

One of the most difficult parts of this process has been finding the courage to trust again. I truly believed I could trust this staff person when I opened up to him. After all, he had encouraged me to talk to him about my goals. He was the one who wanted to hear my hopes and dreams for ministry, and he had the authority to help catapult them forward.

One of the passions I shared with him was forming a supportive community for artists — musicians, writers, painters, sculptors, whatevers. If it was art to you, it was art to me. The community we lived in at the time didn't have much to offer artists. So I had a dream to open a gallery and café within our church. We had the space to do it — and the money as well.

After sharing my idea with this person, he gave me the OK to pursue it completely, as long as it didn't interfere with my daily responsibilities. I spent countless sleepless nights drawing out plans, writing a proposal and a mission statement. I connected with local musicians and artists, and I spread the vision everywhere I went. I also helped design the room, from picking out colors to visiting other galleries to evaluating lighting options.

One day, the staff member pulled me aside to ask how I thought the process was going. Elated, I told him everything I had been doing. He asked me if I'd like to manage it when it opened up. "Are you kidding me? Yes!" I responded.

He asked me some practical questions too. *Did I have any experience as a barista?* No, but I could learn. *What about experience in retail — did I have any?* Right after high school, I managed a Christian bookstore and loved it. I knew how to inventory and clean and report and manage teams. Plus, we had a ton of passionate volunteers who were willing to chip in.

Then he asked me the million dollar question: *Would you rather manage the gallery or stay in your current position?*

I didn't have to think very long. I had already been thinking about it. I had been praying about it. I had even talked to some friends about it. "If it was going to be a full-time position, I'd love to transition over and take it on," was what I told him.

That answer gave him all the ammunition he needed to shoot that dream right between the eyes.

"What would you do if I didn't let you manage the gallery? Would you quit?"

I was totally confused.

"No. I would continue in what I'm currently doing. If you didn't think I was going to be the right person for that job, I'd trust you'd find the right person. I just want it to be successful, and I can certainly help as a volunteer if I need to."

"Well, it's obvious your heart is not in your current job. It's in this gallery. And I don't think you have the experience to run it. So I'm not going to offer it to you. I think you might want to consider your future on our staff."

Blindsided. *Are you kidding me?*

I wasn't surprised by the fact that he wasn't offering me the job, although it appeared to have been his initial intent in our meeting. I was completely shocked that he had set me up. I told him I would make sure

I'd keep doing a good job in my current position, and I left the meeting before I began bawling in front of him.

From this point on, life as I knew it on this church staff would never be the same. He began telling other staff members that I was performing poorly (even though my review from a few weeks prior had exceeded expectations in several areas). He changed my schedule, which made it difficult to work with the team members I needed to work with. One of the final straws was when he forcefully took over a major project I was responsible for. Even though it was moving along successfully and had the approval of each of the key staff leaders, he verbally declared in a public meeting he was "pulling rank and taking over."

My confidence sunk. Maybe I *was* a terrible performer. Maybe I *wasn't* capable of handling minor decisions. Maybe the gallery idea *was* stupid.

Even I began believing the lies.

So a short time after he took over the project, I "resigned." (You know how that works.)

I may have left my post on staff, but I never stopped believing those lies.

I was terrified to return to ministry. Honestly, I was terrified to return to any kind of job. I questioned my ministry calling. I questioned my leadership capabilities. I questioned my faith.

Over the last several years, I've found it difficult to share my biggest dreams and passions with people. I'm afraid that if I reveal my innermost thoughts, somehow they'll be used against me.

I recently was at a tech conference, and one of my favorite writers, Penelope Trunk, shared some thoughts on life and career. She said something I believe is so true.

"People are afraid to be amazing."

I almost broke down crying right then and there.

Right now? I'm still hurting from that painful experience. I'm afraid to be amazing because I'm afraid to trust again. I know that I haven't yet fully regained the confidence I had several years ago. And I know it's stopping me from allowing God to work in me — for *his* greatness.

Remember, Satan will do anything to beat us down and make us ineffective for the kingdom. This includes warping our perspective on trusting others and ourselves again.

Trusting God

One of the first steps in learning to trust again is realizing that unless we fully trust God and his sovereignty, it will be impossible to trust others. The psalmist writes:

> [A righteous person] will have no fear of bad news,
>> his heart is steadfast, trusting in the LORD.
>
> — Psalm 112:7

When someone betrays your trust, it crushes your heart. The Hebrew word translated "steadfast" is *kûn*, which means "to *be erect*, to *set up* — certain (-ty) confirm, direct, faithfulness, be fixed, be stable."[1] We are promised that when we trust the Lord, our hearts become capable of being fixed and stable — even in those times when we face difficult circumstances.

If you've been hurt and are processing through a time of healing, ask yourself if you are trusting God. If you're not, read through the book of Psalms. You'll find many verses that will remind you of God's faithfulness.[2] *He can be trusted.*

Don't get older; get better: Live realistically. Give generously. Adapt willingly. Trust fearlessly. Rejoice daily.

—Charles Swindoll

Trusting Others

Trusting others is similar to forgiving others in the sense that it's a conscious decision, not a feeling. It involves a willful effort.

Some think that it takes two to dance the dance of trust.

> That trust must be earned.

> > That people must be proven trustworthy over time.

While there is some truth to this (you wouldn't trust a convicted child molester to babysit for you), the Bible talks about trust in a different light. The apostle Paul writes, "[Love] … always trusts" (1 Corinthians 13:7). The kind of love he writes about here is *agapē* love — a sacrificial love that places the needs of others above yourself. You have to be reckless in the way you love, even after you're hurt. And even if you are hurt again.

Learning to Trust Fearlessly

We will continue to experience pain and hurt in life. We'll continue to be betrayed. The truth is, humans are just what they are — human. We make mistakes. You'll be let down, and you will also let down. The key is to trust fearlessly.

How can we trust fearlessly? By knowing that God is protecting us.

> Always.

And the enemy is out to destroy us.

> Always.

When you are tempted to give up on trust, remember truth.

God wants you to dream again.

> God wants you to trust again.

> > Jesus came to give you life.

> > *An abundant life.*

God offers you a life not lacking in anything — including trust.

EPILOGUE: RESTING IN AN ABUNDANT LIFE

"The thief comes only to steal and kill and destroy; I have come that they may have life, and have it to the full."

—John 10:10

Full means complete — but full does not always mean good.

We look for instant fixes. We feel empty, and we want to feel full. God promised us fullness, right? Why don't we sense that completeness? We search for whatever we think will tide us over.

And what we do find is only a cheap fix. It's not what God intended.

The Greek word *perissos* is translated "full" in John 10:10. It doesn't mean happy. It doesn't mean comfortable. It doesn't mean prosperous or wealthy.

> *Perissos* means "in abundance."
> > Overflowing.
> > > Life overflowing.
> > > > Overflowing with what? Well, with life.

Not a long life, or even a healthy one. The life in John 10:10 is the life that was made possible, brought into existence, so to speak, when Jesus sacrificed for us. It's eternal life. And the Greek word for "life" (*zōē*) implies a life that is present now and in the future.

> "I have come" (the work is already done) ...
> > "That they may have"
> > (there's nothing you can do to earn it — so just accept it) ...
> > > "Life."

We need to realize that the abundant life God has for you *already exists*!

It's ours.

We need to rest in that fact.

And I mean *really* rest.

BUT WHAT ABOUT SACRIFICE?

Ministry does require sacrifice. The Christian life requires sacrifice. In his letter to the Romans, Paul writes,

> I urge you, brothers, in view of God's mercy, to offer your bodies as living sacrifices, holy and pleasing to God — this is your spiritual act of worship.
>
> —Romans 12:1

When Jesus died on the cross, the need for Old Testament sacrifices died with him. Jesus is and was and always will be *the* ultimate sacrifice.

God's grace is amazing, and it is beyond my understanding how and why he continues to use us in spite of our frailties. Yet my heart breaks because I believe the church (the church universal) is not doing all we can do. We are not completely offering our individual lives as *holy* and *living* sacrifices.

God has always wanted sacrifices that come from humble hearts that look to him in faith, hearts infused with the new life of the Holy Spirit, hearts transformed to live and love like Jesus. He does not want the sacrifices of those who do not live holy and pleasing lives. The Old Testament prophets make it clear that God would prefer that people don't worship him at all than that they worship him while living a lifestyle of injustice (see Isaiah 1:11 – 17; Amos 5:21 – 24; Malachi 1:10 – 11).

How can we truly offer ourselves as the living sacrifices God requires?

Realize there's a difference between what you feel you must sacrifice and what God actually requires.

The only sacrifice he requires is *you.*
    You to *him.*
We are living sacrifices, holy and pleasing to God.

Offering ourselves up to him *is* our act of worship.
And that is the only sacrifice he requires.

Live and rest fully and abundantly in that promise. His mercy and his grace will take care of the rest.

SABBATH

Many books have been written on the importance of the Sabbath. Countless leadership talks have encouraged us to take appropriate rest. We talk about it, pray about it, and even say we're going to do it — but for the most part, we don't change a thing!

When we think of Sabbath, we think of resting on the seventh day. After all, God took six days to create the world. On the seventh day, he rested. We might think of Sabbath as a reward for our hard work.

However, let me challenge you to think of Sabbath in a different way.

First, we need to recognize that God didn't *need* to rest. He is God. But he rested anyway. He created human beings with a need for a day in which they could step aside from the busyness and the mundane in order to refocus and be restored. God created all things, and then took a day of rest, knowing he was setting the ultimate example.

In *Sit, Walk, Stand*, Watchman Nee describes the Sabbath:

> Where did [Adam] stand in relation to that rest of God? Adam, we are told, was created on the sixth day. Clearly, then, he had no part in those first six days of work, for he came into being only at their end. God's seventh day was, in fact, Adam's first. Where God worked six days and then enjoyed his Sabbath rest, Adam began his life with the Sabbath; for God works before he rests, while man must first enter into God's rest, and then alone can he work.[3]

The New Testament often uses the word *rest* to describe the good news of grace and salvation proclaimed in Jesus Christ (see, for example, Matthew 11:28; Hebrews 4:2 – 3).[4] So the Sabbath doesn't just signify a day of rest but defines why we are able to rest, and *should* rest, because of the connection to the gospel. Salvation itself begins in rest — knowing that Jesus has already accomplished perfection in his life and death. We can only truly rest by realizing we have been made complete in Jesus Christ. The Sabbath isn't only referring to one particular day in the seven days of the week. It also points to our entering into God's eternal rest, where kingdom work has already been accomplished.

Watchman Nee continues:

> And here is the gospel: that God has gone one stage further and has completed also the work of redemption, and that we need to do nothing whatever to merit it, but can enter by faith directly into the values of his finished work.[5]

If you think that wanting to keep busy all the time is a product of modern-day technology, take a look at what the prophet Isaiah declared:

> This is what the Sovereign Lord, the Holy One of Israel, says:
>
> "In repentance and rest is your salvation,
>> in quietness and trust is your strength,
>> but you would have none of it."
>
> — Isaiah 30:15

Even thousands of years ago, mankind refused the beautiful gift of rest. Why do we always prefer the opposite? In fact, please allow me the liberty of flipping this verse into its opposite form.

> "In rebellion and work is your demise,
>> in noisiness and distrust is your weakness,
>> and you will have it all the time."

Why do those words ring so true?

Because we are believing lies!

We believe lies that tell us that our worth is in our productivity. We believe lies that say you can't trust anybody with your problems. We are so tempted by the glitz and glamour of sacrifice and doing things for

Christ that we ignore the work Christ has already done in us. We allow false humility and large egos to drive us into eighty-hour weeks and an unholy commitment to self-reliance.

And when we are relying on ourselves, we aren't relying on God.

Self-reliance quietly whispers to our souls, "You don't need rest. You don't need to refresh. You can do everything on your own. God is helping you, right?"

In Mark 6, Jesus sends the apostles out two by two to do his work. It was one of those "all hands on deck" kind of seasons. They were incredibly busy, incredibly hurried. And even as they filed their report with Jesus, there was such a hustle and bustle of activity around them that they didn't have a chance to eat.

Busy? Hurried? Skipping meals?

Yep. Sounds like ministry.

And they pushed through.

After spending some time with Jesus, instead of heading straight back into their ministry, they are commanded to rest.

"Come with me by yourselves to a quiet place and get some rest" (Mark 6:31).

We cannot be dependent on ourselves and on God at the same time. When we consider the practice of rest unnecessary, we will also inevitably lose sight of the necessity of God.

—Anne Jackson

Jesus knew that the apostles needed to rest.

Alone.

But at the same time — *with him.*

Jesus is telling you to come to him to find rest. You don't need a burning bush. He tells you through Scripture. He tells you through circumstances and people. He speaks this invitation to you when your soul is empty and your heart can't take anymore.

You need rest.

As I mentioned in chapter 4, I took a trip to Uganda with Compassion International. It was the most difficult and rewarding experience of my life so far. We arrived at 12:30 a.m., and after traveling for almost thirty hours, I was able to sleep a couple of hours before heading out with the team to visit a variety of child-development projects, meet church leaders, and play with children living in poverty.

The trip became more and more intense as the days went on. We visited a project focused on child survival. We made formula of diluted milk, olive oil, and grain for babies. We hugged teenage mothers and carried around toddlers. The next day, we visited one of the only HIV/AIDS-focused hospitals in the world. Children ran and played, oblivious to their imminent fate (something that haunted us all); the ones closest to death lay still in beds in open-air rooms, their atrophied arms pierced by life-giving needles and fluids.

With each day, our unusually extroverted group grew more solemn. And our trip leaders knew that this kind of reaction would happen. With little sleep, lots of spiritual warfare, and the contrast of death and hope, poverty and richness, and war and love surrounding us, they knew we would need to decompress.

They knew we would need to rest.

After three solid days of intense experiences, we took a small plane (an intense experience in and of itself) to a spot about 250 miles away from Kampala, the country's largest city. The lodge at which we were staying was powered by a generator. The nearest medical facility was six hours away on unpaved and potentially unsafe roads.

We were in the middle of nowhere.

And it was time to rest.

One afternoon, we took a ferry across the Nile River and then hopped into a small bus. We drove for a half hour on the bumpiest dirt road one could imagine before coming to Murchison Falls, one of the many wonders of the world. We then hiked another half hour to the very top.

Slowly we progressed on a narrow, rocky trail, dodging tree branches and mosquitoes along the way. We occasionally stopped at the most beautiful parts of the rapids, taking pictures of each other, but for the most part, the hike remained the quietest part of the trip.

As we reached the top of the falls, we passed several signs warning us of the steep cliffs and the danger that awaited. Nobody was scared. Everyone was in awe. We helped each other over the slippery rocks and finally reached the very top.

They say many people have died at Murchison Falls. There are no railings to stop you from falling over. It's you, the rocks, and the falls. The beauty of water is transformed into something breathtaking. People become mesmerized by the unique blend of tranquility and power. Standing as close to the edge as our leaders and guides would let us, we let the wind-carried spray slowly drench us. Any fears of falling, of accidentally swallowing the parasite-infested water, of getting ravished by malaria-carrying mosquitoes — those fears had all vanished.

The hardships of the trip — the pain we saw, the poverty, the brokenness — those things didn't disappear or float away in the rapids of the Nile. But taking a day to rest — to go to a quiet place and be reminded of the incredible power of the Creator — made me fall even more in awe of his sovereignty and his ultimate message of hope.

Rest bound together the incomplete to the complete.

We were refreshed. Inspired. Re-created. And we were able to rest in the knowledge and grace that, although there are many things for us to do, we are already a part of "on earth as it is in heaven."

Rest.

It is that simple command.

Humble.

Concerned.

Wise.

Loving.

"Come with me by yourselves to a quiet place and get some rest."

And rest, knowing that the work is already made complete by a cross, and that you belong to a Savior who wants nothing more for you than to live a fully abundant life.

It's your turn.

Go with him. Alone.

To a quiet place.

And rest.

I value your thoughts about what you've just read.
Please share them with me. You'll find contact information
in the back of this book.

Chapter 1: Comparing Mad Cow Disease to Mad Church Disease

1. See Centers for Disease Control and Prevention, "BSE (Bovine Spongiform Encephalopathy, or Mad Cow Disease)," http://www.cdc.gov/ncidod/dvrd/bse/.

Chapter 2: The Emergency

1. Ellison Research, "Exclusive Findings from Ellison Research," http://www.ellisonresearch.com/PublicStudies.htm.

2. Apollo Health online, "Sleep Statistics," http://www.apollolight.com/sleep_stats.html.

3. Ellison Research, "Just How Healthy Is the Typical Pastor?" http://www.ellisonresearch.com/releases/20030801.htm.

4. Ibid.

5. Craig Groeschel, "Lessons from My Kids 2 (of 5)," http://swerve.lifechurch.tv/2007/10/page/2/.

6. Ellison Research, "New Research Shows Pastors May Not Have a Realistic View of the Health of Their Own Family," http://www.ellisonresearch.com/ERPS%20II/release_17_family.htm.

7. Thanks, Wes Hamilton, for calling attention to this book on your Facebook. Please read this book with caution. You can view *Preacher and Prayer* online at http://www.thecorner-stone.org/preacher_prayer_1.html.

8. See Ellison Research, "Study Shows Only 16% of Protestant Ministers Are Very Satisfied with Their Personal Prayer Lives," http://www.ellisonresearch.com/ERPS%20II/release_16_prayer.htm.

9. Excerpt from Bounds, *Preacher and Prayer*, chapter 1, http://www.thecorner-stone.org/preacher_prayer_1.html.

Chapter 3: Internal Risk Factors

1. See Meyer Friedman and Ray H. Rosenman, *Type A Behavior and Your Heart* (New York: Knopf, 1974).

Chapter 5: Symptoms

1. Archibald Hart, "Depressed, Stressed, and Burned Out: What's Going On in My Life?" *Enrichment Journal*, http://enrichmentjournal. ag.org/200603/200603_020_burnout.cfm.

Chapter 6: Five Principles of Recovery

1. W. E. Vine, *Vine's Complete Expository Dictionary of Old and New Testament Words* (Nashville: Nelson, 1996), 525.

Chapter 7: Spiritual Health

1. For a very helpful framework, see the discussion on the discipline of service in Richard Foster, *Celebration of Discipline* (New York: Harper & Row, 1978), 111 – 13. The comparisons in the chart are adapted from Foster's book.

Chapter 8: Physical Health

1. Wellness International Network, "Obesity Statistics," http://web. winltd.com/Article.aspx?PageURL=/Pages/English/healthnews/ obesitystats.htm.

2. Mayo Clinic, "Exercise: Rev Up Your Routine to Reduce Stress," http:// www.mayoclinic.com/health/exercise-and-stress/SR00036.

3. Gary Kinnaman and Richard Jacobs, *Seeing in the Dark: Getting the Facts on Depression and Finding Hope Again* (Minneapolis: Bethany, 2006).

4. See Wikipedia, "Sleep Deprivation," http://en.wikipedia.org/wiki/ Sleep_deprivation.

5. For helpful information about sleep issues, see Better Health Channel, "Fact Sheet: Sleep Deprivation," http://www.betterhealth.vic.gov.au/ bhcv2/bhcpdf.nsf/ByPDF/Sleep_deprivation/$File/Sleep_deprivation. pdf ; Postgraduate Medicine Online, "Patient Notes: Sleep Deprivation," http://www.postgradmed.com/issues/2002/10_02/pn_sleep.shtml; Franklin Institute Online, "The Human Brain: Sleep and Stress," http:// www.fi.edu/learn/brain/sleep.html.

Chapter 10: Relational Health

1. Shankar Vedantam, "Social Isolation Growing in U.S., Study Says," http://www.washingtonpost.com/wp-dyn/content/article/2006/06/22/ AR2006062201763 pf.html.

2. See James S. House, "Social Isolation Kills, But How and Why?" *Psychosomatic Medicine* 63 (2001): 273 – 74, http://www. psychosomaticmedicine.org/cgi/content/full/63/2/273#R1-087713.

Chapter 11: Processing through Pain

1. James Strong, *The New Strong's Complete Dictionary of Bible Words* (Nashville: Nelson, 1996), #3559, p. 401.

2. Here are some places to begin: Psalm 9:10; 22:4 – 5; 32:10; 37:3 – 6; 91; 118:6 – 9; 125:1 – 2.

3. Watchman Nee, *Sit, Walk, Stand* (Downers Grove, Ill.: Tyndale, 1977), 16.

4. For a good overview, see the online article "The Sabbath Rest," http:// www.gospel-herald.com/sabbath_studies/sabbath_rest.htm.

5. Nee, *Sit, Walk, Stand*, 16.

ACKNOWLEDGMENTS

It would be incredibly sad if I wrote a book about burnout and burned out in the process. For this very reason, I must give serious props and love to my husband, Chris. Chris, you have helped me realize how to relax and embrace this precious gift we've been given called time. Your hope inspires me, and your leadership moves me. Thank you for — well, everything. I love you more than chocolate.

To my family, I can't thank you enough for always supporting me regardless of how outlandish my dreams have been and for giving me a hand when those dreams have gotten me in trouble. Your courage in ministry has shown me that the beauty of the church is something worth fighting for.

In the last several years of ministry, I have been blessed and honored to have so many amazing people cross my path. It would be impossible to list everyone, so I do ask for your grace if I don't mention you, and I hope I've expressed my gratitude to you before.

A tribe is essential to survival. Crystal Renaud, Andrew Shepherd, Julie Trasp, Kristi "Applesauce" Fair, Lynse Stevens, Spence Smith, the Bergstroms, and the Havens — your support and love and encouragement have pushed me forward on this path.

To the staff and people of Cross Point Community Church in Nashville: thank you for your friendship and for giving me the freedom to carry out all the dreams God has planted in my heart. It is my greatest wish that I will encourage your God-given dreams as well.

Those of you who call LifeChurch.tv, Lake Pointe Church, and Westside Family Church your home: I have been richly blessed to have served hand in hand with you.

This book would still be an idea in my head if it weren't for the generous action and support of Terry Storch, Craig Groeschel, Bobby Gruenewald,

Seth Godin, Kurt Bruner, Mary DeMuth, David Kinnaman, Eric Bryant, Joe Louthan, and Ashley Wiersma. Thanks for taking a risk on me.

To my Deadly Viper cohorts, Mike Foster and Jud Wilhite: it is an honor to fight assassins with you.

To my new friends at Catalyst: you guys are so talented and creative. What you are letting God do through your passion is nothing short of amazing.

Several gracious leaders contributed to this book with their wisdom and insight, and others boldly shared stories with me. Thank you for letting the world into your life, your pain, and your hope.

Beth Jusino: you are more than an agent — you are a friend, a dreamer, and a lifesaver. Thank you. And the team at Zondervan: your faith in me, as well as your commitment to the church (and grammar), makes me proud to partner with you.

The Rest of God, Mark Buchanan's incredible book on Sabbath rest, has reshaped the way I think about rest, and I highly recommend that you read it.

My fellow Compassion International bloggers — your friendship as we crossed oceans and continents (and fought off Ugandan bats) has truly changed my life.

And last, but certainly not least — to every person who has ever been a part of the community on FlowerDust.net, who has supported this book during this long and amazing process: the words "thank you" do not express the depth of my appreciation. With your stories and your encouragement, this book has come to life.

VISIT MADCHURCHDISEASE.COM FOR MORE STORIES AND TO SHARE YOUR OWN

THE PERCEIVED EXPECTATIONS OF OTHERS, THE STRESS THAT IT CAN CAUSE AND THE FINANCIAL STRAIN CAUSED BY SUCH A LOW SALARY AND NO BENEFITS.

PERSONAL CIRCUMSTANCES AND UNREALISTIC EXPECTATIONS FROM CHURCH MEMBERS

CHURCH ATTENDANCE/ WORSHIP BECOMES MORE OF A JOB THAN A DESIRE TO SERVE GOD BECAUSE OF WHO HE IS.

I GREW UP IN A PASTOR'S HOME AND THOUGHT I WOULD WANT THIS - I DO NOT LIKE KNOWING THE INNER-WORKINGS OF A CHURCH AND I GET "BURNED" BY THE CHURCH OFTEN.

THE TIME AWAY FROM HOME, AWAY FROM FAMILY, AND JUST THAT IT'S ALWAYS ABOUT THE MINISTRY. WE CAN'T ESCAPE IT. BEING THE "MINISTER'S WIFE."

TIME—EVERYONE ELSE COMES FIRST

LONELINESS, CRITICISM, EXPECTATIONS

SEEING YOUR PARNER GET HURT OVER AND OVER AGAIN

THEY COULD VOTE US OUT, THEY COULD LEAVE THE CHURCH, THEY COULD GOSSIP ABOUT US, THEY COULD STOP PAYING US.

THAT I AM RELEGATED TO CHIEF COOK AND BOTTLE WASHER

FLIRTING

HYPOCRISY

FEMALES

LIVING BEING

SEEING THE BACKEND OF THE CHURCH BUSINESS, I GET TO SEE WHAT MOST DON'T, AND THEY SHOULD BE GLAD THEY DON'T

REALIZING THAT PEOPLE HIDE BEHIND GOD AS AN EXCUSE FOR FORCED SEXISM IN MINISTRY

THE LACK OF BEING ABLE TO PRIORITIZE THE CHURCH HOME

FEELING LIKE MY WHOLE LIFE AND FAMILY ARE AN OPEN BOOK FOR EVERYONE ELSE IN THE CHURCH... NO PRIVACY!!!

IT'S NEVER OFF. "CHURCH" IS ALWAYS ON. WE ARE TALKING ABOUT IT IF WE ARE NOT AT IT.

THERE IS NO ONE TO FILL OUR CUP BACK UP AGAIN AS WE ALWAYS GIVE OF OURSELVES.

PEOPLE CAN BE DEMANDING AND EXHAUSTING.

ALL TOO OFTEN IT'S DIFFICULT TO SEPARATE OUR SPIRITUAL LIVES FROM OUR CHURCH LIFE.

ALL THE NASTY, CRITICAL PEOPLE HE HAS TO MINISTER TO

THE RESPONSIBILITY OF ALWAYS BEING IN CHARGE. NEVER GETTING TO BE MINISTERED TO

WE SACRIFICE VIRTUALLY EVERY WEEKEND OF THE YEAR, AS HUSBAND AND WIFE WE DON'T HAVE ANY DAYS OFF DURING THE WEEK TOGETHER.

I OFTEN HAVE TO SHARE MY HUSBAND WITH SO MANY PEOPLE WHO WANT A PIECE OF HIM.

NO RESPECT, GRATITUDE, OR EVEN ACKNOWLEDGMENT FROM THE ELDERSHIP FOR THE SACRIFICES OUR ENTIRE FAMILY MADE SO THAT MY HUSBAND COULD GIVE HIS BEST TO HIS JOB

HAVING TO GO TO CHURCH OUT OF OBLIGATION INSTEAD OF GOING BECAUSE I WANT TO

BEING IN MINISTRY OFTEN MEANS NOT BEING ABLE TO TALK ABOUT REGULAR JOB STRESS WITH YOUR FRIENDS. THIS OFTEN BECOMES OVERWHELMING.

IT WAS IMPOSSIBLE TO PLEASE THE PASTOR

EVERYONE CONSTANTLY HAS SOMETHING TO SAY ABOUT YOU. THEY CRITICIZE EVERYTHING ABOUT YOUR FAMILY, DOES, EVEN WHEN

Share Your Thoughts

With the Author: Your comments will be forwarded to
the author when you send them to *zauthor@zondervan.com*.

With Zondervan: Submit your review of this book
by writing to *zreview@zondervan.com*.

Free Online Resources at
www.zondervan.com/hello

 Zondervan AuthorTracker: Be notified whenever your favorite authors publish new books, go on tour, or post an update about what's happening in their lives.

 Daily Bible Verses and Devotions: Enrich your life with daily Bible verses or devotions that help you start every morning focused on God.

 Free Email Publications: Sign up for newsletters on fiction, Christian living, church ministry, parenting, and more.

 Zondervan Bible Search: Find and compare Bible passages in a variety of translations at www.zondervanbiblesearch.com.

 Other Benefits: Register yourself to receive online benefits like coupons and special offers, or to participate in research.